Contemporary

MW00895267

CONTENTS

Editorial

Contemporary Women Poets

FEMINIST REVIEW NO 62, SUMMER 1999, ISSN 0141-7789, PP. 1–5

My aim in compiling this issue of *Feminist Review* has been to produce a series of articles that are accessible and informative to a non-specialist reader. With this in mind, I commissioned essays on broad themes, rather than opting for the more detailed discussion of individual poets that is common in literary studies. *Feminist Review* has a multidisciplinary readership, and I wanted to address this audience explicitly. I also hoped to show that, contrary to common assumptions, a society's poetry is extremely closely connected to its values, beliefs and political debates. I thus chose to focus on aspects of contemporary poetry that either directly engage with, or indirectly raise some of the preoccupations that are evident in recent feminist thought. All the contributors currently live in Britain (which is not to suggest they regard themselves as 'British'); as a result, these articles reflect the present situation in poetry from that geographical position. But poetry crosses borders, and I hope the international origins of those represented in these pages, as well as the wide relevance of their subject-matter, will resonate with poets and critics from other parts of the world.

In the early 1980s, at least five anthologies of poetry by women appeared, published at first by the women's presses, later by mainstream publishers who realized there was money to be made.[1] Despite some lukewarm reactions, this burst of activity probably played an important part in encouraging more women to write. Today most commentators acknowledge the presence and achievement of a large number of women poets; some even suggest that more women are being published than ever before. Personally, I have anxieties about the permanence of these writers' impact and reputations. Research suggests that, in their own time, women have often been extremely successful poets, but they slip out of literary history, rarely making it into the official canon of 'great' literature. However, there are certainly lots of talented and determined women writing, publishing and performing poetry today – cause for great celebration. As a result, there is some feeling, which echoes that more generally abroad, that the 'battle'

FEMINIST REVIEW NO 62, SUMMER 1999

has been won. With women in positions of power and influence (publishing, giving readings, winning prizes), why keep talking of inequality, or the significance of gender?

My own feeling is that women are now visible participants, but the poetry world's institutions (both those overseeing the editing and publishing of collections, magazines and journals, and those institutions producing academic debate about poetry) – its codes of interpretation and evaluation – remains unaltered and largely unaffected by their presence. Women poets want to be judged by the same standards as their male colleagues; there is great – understandable – fear of special treatment, because it has traditionally meant relegation to the women's poetic sphere, associated with sentiment(-ality), personal feelings and narrowness in range and daring. Bold declarations made in the 1980s about the need for a new, feminist aesthetic never resulted in any clear outline or example, and this is a vacuum that, as Jane Dowson suggests in her essay here, urgently needs filling. As a result, the profoundly gendered workings of poetry creation, reception and interpretation remain concealed.

A decade ago, I think that such initiatives were widely misunderstood. It was assumed that critics who urged the need for new aesthetic criteria intended to junk literary tradition and abandon conventional attentiveness to, and respect for language, form and rhythm.[2] A lot of the poetry published expressed attitudes and experience validated by the Women's Movement, and there was a clear political impetus behind the act of publishing it: women speaking out publicly, and breaking into previously male arenas like the small and elite world of poetry. Several high-profile poets distanced themselves from this work, and therefore from any effort to articulate a female poetic tradition, or to group poets on the basis of sex. As a result of this stalemate, the term 'feminist poetry' emerged, and with it the unhelpfully reductive implication that a feminist critical approach to poetry entailed a narrow and literalist focus on subject matter, accompanied by complete indifference to any other aspect of the poem.

Most general surveys of twentieth-century poetry now include a well-intentioned chapter on 'women poets', but it does not go much beyond a rather tame listing of themes.[3] This is thin progress when female names are almost entirely absent from the whole of the rest of the book, and when 'general' anthologies – *The New British Poetry* (Bloodaxe, 1993); *The Penguin Book of Poetry from Britain and Ireland since 1945* (1998) – still select an insultingly small number of women. We need critiques that explore poets' use of personae, form and figurative language; that consider the lyric's ancient tradition alongside its present pre-eminence, and that attempt to revive other subgenres like narrative and epic poetry.

The articles that follow, as I have already indicated, are more general in approach. The influence of poststructuralism in poetry is acknowledged in Harriet Tarlo's introduction to experimental language poetry, non-representational writing that makes imaginative use of recent feminist theoretical work as well as of Modernism's neglected legacy. Liz Yorke finds that the idea of a lesbian poetics is as troublesomely complex as all identity politics today. Tensions in cross-generational relationships between women poets form an important theme in Jane Dowson's examination of literary history and women's curious absence from it. There is a long round-table discussion with Jean Binta Breeze, Patience Agbabi and Jillian Tipene. Poetry in performance has become very popular recently, generating big audiences and often marking a fruitful cross-fertilization between African, Caribbean, English and American traditions in both music and poetry. The work of poets like Linton Kwesi Johnson and Jean Breeze has been extremely influential, but very little has been published about it. In the transcript of this meeting, specially commissioned by *Feminist Review*, fascinating details emerge about the politics and economics of working as a poet. As well as covering poets and poetry, I also wanted to include some recognition of the therapeutic value of the genre. I was impressed by Survivors' Poetry, a national organization supporting workshops and performances by and for survivors of the mental health system.[4] Gillie Bolton's article gives a sense of the potential offered by poetry-writing within therapeutic contexts, and also of the range of initiatives currently underway in the British Isles.

Finally, poet Sarah Maguire revisits an influential essay published by Irish poet Eavan Boland in 1986. Boland, like Adrienne Rich, identified a tension between the role of poet and that of woman. Rich located it in a potential clash between 'the energy of creation and the energy of relation'; Boland described a 'psychosexual pressure'. While Maguire argues that much has changed, she also suggests that women poets' work 'is still inflected (and infected) by inequalities and by our objectified subjectivity'. To me, there is a further (related) issue: confidence. This involves the necessity for self-belief; taking one's art seriously, making time for it, keeping faith with it and in it, through times of rejection and silence. Contemporary feminist debate seems to avoid this issue, as if it is too simple, or embarrassingly dated; as though none of us have faltering confidence any longer. In addition, the role of the poet, and its associations with authority, with the position of spokesperson, may create more difficulties. Partly, I suspect, as writers women may find that role inappropriate or uncomfortable; and in terms of poetry's reception, I think many men (and probably many women too) are instinctively resistant to the idea of accepting a woman speaking on their behalf, as their spokesperson. It is easy to accept her if

FEMINIST REVIEW NO 62, SUMMER 1999

she speaks for a community of women, but for society, for everyone? As I have argued elsewhere,[5] a female voice is not easily accepted as 'universal', ungendered (or, as is usually the case, male but ostensibly sex-neutral). The only way to tackle this is to get women's voices alongside men's, so they are not in a minority, and can no longer appear aberrant or partial.

Finally, a word on the poems. I wish there were more; there aren't because I chose to include a very long poem about her daughter by Mimi Khalvati. I like the idea of such large-scale projects, and wanted to encourage women to undertake them – to venture out of the brief lyric, to try something bigger. To me this is – once again – to do with laying claim to importance and suggests greater confidence.

So a mixture of joy and scepticism. Women are out there at performances and readings; they attend conferences, workshops and festivals yet, in my experience, they stay very quiet in mixed company. We urgently need women editors. We also need women readers and critics. Not because 'women' form a cohesive group in any easy way; not because such a thing as 'women's poetry', with its unhelpful implications of uniformity, exists, but precisely because we don't and it doesn't. If this issue of *Feminist Review* encourages any of these activities, it will have performed the most useful service I can imagine.

Vicki Bertram
School of Humanities
Oxford Brookes University

Notes

1 See 'Poetry and the Women's Movement in Postwar Britain' by Claire Buck in Acheson and Huk (eds) *Contemporary British Poetry: Essays in Theory and Criticism* (State University of New York, 1996), 81–112; also 'Anthologies of Women's Poetry: Canon-Breakers; Canon:Makers', by Jane Dowson, 237–52, and 'Women Poets and "Women's Poetry": Fleur Adcock, Gillian Clarke and Carol Rumens' by Lyn Pykett, 253–67, both in Day and Docherty (eds), *British Poetry from the 1950s to the 1990s: Politics and Art* (Macmillan, 1997).

2 See Eavan Boland's 'The Woman Poet: Her Dilemma', first published in *Stand* (1986), reprinted in *Object Lessons: The Life of the Woman and the Poet in our Time* (Vintage, 1996). Also, see Carol Rumens' introduction to *Making for the Open: The Chatto Book of Post-feminist Poetry, 1964–84* (Chatto & Windus, 1985).

3 Examples include Alan Robinson, *Instabilities in Contemporary British Poetry*

(Macmillan, 1988) and Peter Childs, *The Twentieth Century in Poetry* (Routledge, 1999), which is heavily dependent on Robinson's account.

4 Survivors' Poetry is funded by the Arts Council and the Mental Health Foundation. They have regional groups across the country, and support training, networking and publication ventures. They are based at Diorama Arts Centre, 34 Osnaburgh Street, London NW1 3ND; tel: 0171 916 5317.

5 See 'Postfeminist Poetry? "one more word for balls" ', 269–292 in Huk and Acheson, *Contemporary British Poetry: Essays in Theory and Criticism* (SUNY, 1996).

'Older Sisters Are Very Sobering Things':
Contemporary Women Poets and the Female Affiliation Complex

Jane Dowson

FEMINIST REVIEW NO 62, SUMMER 1999, ISSN 0141-7789, PP. 6–20

Abstract

If, as history indicates, the directions of poetry are determined by its inheritance – that is, its perception of its past – in looking at literary records such as poems, reviews and other critical texts, it is possible to anticipate how twentieth-century women's poetry will come to be defined and the extent to which it will have value and authority. This in its turn will formulate the nature and status of women's poetry in the twenty-first century. In surveying twentieth-century poetry in Britain, the signs are that just as the label 'poetess' was a handicap to the self-perception of a woman at the beginning of this century, so the label 'woman poet' will shackle her in the next, largely because her end-of-the-twentieth-century predecessors will have become mythologized as a literary underclass, undermined and overlooked. One reason for the pattern of the last three hundred years, where women publish and then slip from literary histories, is that they do not receive proper attention from male-dominated literary criticism. Although women now seem to be sufficiently published to make segregation unnecessary, there is still a case for positive discrimination or their names will disappear from the records. Positive discrimination in the form of gendered segregation is, however, opposed by poets because of their uneasy relationship with one another. Women poets need an alternative line of development to the 'masculinity complex' whereby they unsuccessfully seek recognition within the male traditions, or the 'female affiliation complex' which prevents them from identifying themselves with one another. It will be argued that there is an emerging tendency in recent poets to plunder and appropriate the associations of the male tradition and that feminist critics need to theorize this aesthetic and make connections between poets so that they become positive role models for poets of the future.

Keywords

contemporary women's poetry; twentieth-century womens' poetry; women poets; future of women's poetry; female affiliation complex; poetry criticism

According to Germaine Greer, 'each generation spawns its scores of women poets who will be dumped by the succeeding generation, even before they are dead' (Greer, 1995b: 8), and she believes that her contemporaries are no exception:

> Hundreds of good women poets now travel the length and breadth of our world, performing their work with wit and style. Their verse does not incessantly vibrate at the highest frequency; they have other subjects besides themselves; they do not see themselves as outcast and solitary or unique in their capacity to be miserable. Because they fail to flay themselves alive, they will be called minor, and forgotten as all but two or three of Squire's[1] contemporary poets have been forgotten.
>
> (Greer, 1995a: 424)

By comparing the concepts of the early twentieth-century 'poetess' and the end of the century woman poet, I shall argue that, in spite of its provocative rhetoric, Greer's warning has to be taken seriously for three reasons. One is that it is informed by the pattern of the last three centuries, which is that women publish, gain esteem and are then dropped from literary records. The second is that myths about the nature of women's poetry as hysterical, melancholy, solipsistic and technically inferior, are persistent – Greer reinforces them through denial here. The third reason is that in *Slipshod Sibyls: Recognition, Rejection and the Woman Poet*, Greer is displaying symptoms of what Gilbert and Gubar call the 'female affiliation complex' (Gilbert and Gubar, 1988: 168); by rubbishing women of the past, and by implication of the present too, she shores up her own credentials as one of the boys, clever and worthy of an enduring place in history. If verdicts like Greer's go unchallenged, women poets will continue to be homogenized and mythologized in ways which prejudice the perception and self-perception of poets; in the absence of positive role models, women in the twenty-first century will dissociate themselves from their twentieth-century predecessors in the same way that women at the beginning of the century wrote in opposition to the derided nineteenth-century poetesses.

The lack of positive models is both a reason for and a consequence of the way in which women are belittled and ignored by the literary establishment, then sidelined and omitted from literary histories. Furthermore, the uncomfortable relationship between women poets, which has gone on throughout this century, is both a cause and effect of the continuing difficulty in formulating a satisfactory critical terminology for reading women's poetry. I shall discuss the three issues identified above as an agenda for feminist critics, if they are to secure women poets a place in literary histories: to be aware that publishing needs to be accompanied by due critical recognition; to conquer the female affiliation complex by providing positive role models; and to counter the myths about women poets by celebrating their diversity but also by making connections between them.

The disappearance of women from this century's histories demonstrates that successful publishing alone is no guarantee of recognition in the future. As Germaine Greer states, the poets in J. C. Squire's anthology, *A Book of Women's Verse* (1921), are now largely unknown, but his observations could describe the current climate: 'With thousands of women writing, with women's verses in every magazine and women represented in every newspaper office . . . we take composition for granted as a feminine occupation' (Squire, 1921: Introduction). However, women also win prizes – seven out of nine on the latest Forward First Collection Prize shortlist were women – but women have always won prizes this century.[2] When it comes to literary histories or anthologies, there is less certainty about women's poetry being judged on equal terms. For all their successes in publishing and winning prizes, women are still under-represented in anthologies – 23 out of 271 poets in *The School Bag* (Heaney and Hughes, 1997) are women – and it is these anthologies which shape the literary consciousness of present and future readers. Additionally, women are still under-represented in the literary journals which will be taken by next century's scholars as the significant records of the contemporary scene. Open any literary paper – apart from *Poetry Review,* which is a self-conscious and encouraging exception – for evidence that a male-dominated critical establishment hogs about 85 per cent of reviews and continues to patronize women. Peter Forbes cites Derek Mahon in the *Irish Times,* ' "Must it be said that, for all the trumpeting about women poets, the empress has no clothes?" ', and comments, 'You don't often meet such totally unreconstructed males these days, but presumably he is only saying what many male poets mutter into their beer' (Forbes, 1996/7: 3). As Maura Dooley observes in her introduction to the newest women-only anthology, *Making for Planet Alice* (1997),

> Women are published, read and heard, but their work is not discussed. Until their work is considered and written about consistently, seriously and undifferentiatingly by the major literary journals of the day, their poetry will not have a future as part of the main canon of English Literature.
>
> (Dooley, 1997: 12)

A *TLS* review described Carol Ann Duffy's use of italics to construct a demotic idiom, as 'lean[ing] towards the demonstrative and the hysterical' (Sansom, 1995: 20). This instance of undermining is revealing because Duffy would appear to have won the respect of her male colleagues. The tone of this criticism makes one question whether she has sufficiently appropriate literary records to be certain of recognition in the future. Duffy represents many contemporary poets in her denouncement, 'I hate that expression, "woman poet". It's as though we were a separate section . . . We are reviewed together in the newspapers, while the men are treated individually' (Duffy, 1990: 61). Her antipathy to labelling by gender is significant because it is a result of the negative treatment by reviewers and because it echoes the complaints of women in the past who have since been sidelined.

I am not going to tour bad reviews and exclusions, important though such statistics are to stop us from ignoring Germaine Greer's gloomy forecast, but instead to investigate their effect on *women's* ambivalence towards one another's reputation, status and creativity. At the beginning of the century, Edith Sitwell was not like Elizabeth Barrett Browning who looked in vain for grandmothers, but nevertheless lamented that there was no adequate female model 'to point the way. I had to learn everything – learn, amongst other things, not to be timid, and that was one of the most difficult things of all.'[3] Her notorious declamation, 'Women's poetry with the exception of Sappho, . . . *Goblin Market* and a few deep and concentrated but fearfully incomplete poems of Emily Dickinson is simply *awful* . . . incompetent, floppy, whining, arch, trivial, self-pitying',[4] reiterated the negative connotations of women's poetry which were perpetuated by the anxious reaction in men to militant women's suffrage. In the context of an intense period of legislation concerning the rights and opportunities of women, the denigration of women's poetry can be seen as a symptom of male resistance to women's entry into the professions and public places; the obsessive labelling of women as 'poetesses', the embodiments of femininity, was a strategy for keeping them in the realm of the personal and domestic. There are many records of women disaffiliating themselves from these mythologies, such as Amy Lowell's comment in 'The Sisters' (1925): 'Taking us by and large, we're a queer lot/We women who write poetry'. In this poem she constructs a dreamstate where the poet meets the stereotypes of her literary matrilineage: the impulsive Sappho, the sickly Mrs Browning whose heart 'Was squeezed in stiff conventions' and the elusive Emily Dickinson who lost her identity through masking it for too long. She cannot identify with any of these 'sisters' – 'I cannot write like you' – but nevertheless she is haunted by them:

> Although you leave me sad and self-distrustful,
> For older sisters are very sobering things.
> Put on your cloaks, my dears, the motor's waiting.
> No, you have not seemed strange to me, but near,
> Frightfully near and rather terrifying.[5]

Contemporary women articulate the same sense of exclusion from a masculine tradition and alienation from their feminine poetic inheritance as women at the start of the twentieth century. In 'Pulse', Jane Holland is conscious of her gendered identity but refutes the label 'woman poet' because of the expectation that she should be limited to women-only concerns:

Why should I speak of motherhood?
I might as well describe breathing
and have done with it.
. . .
I am not a woman poet.
I am a woman and a poet.
The difference is in the eyes.[6]

In 'A Bookshop Revisited', Carol Rumens expresses a debilitating preoccupation with whether women should disguise or proclaim a gendered perspective in their poems:

Women are often glad to be one of the crowd
    And not special cases.
But some would argue there's still a place for proud
    Self-proclaimed poetesses.
. . .
Poet or poetess, we've surely known times
    We sat up all night
In our Yeatsian masks, like good little androgynes,
    And couldn't write.[7]

The above extracts support Gilbert and Gubar's theory of the female affiliation complex, and its associated male reaction formation. They account for women's competing desires to both identify with and be separate from a segregated female tradition in Freudian terms: the pre-Oedipal mother–daughter relationship and the castration complex (Gilbert and Gubar, 1988: 168). Freud describes three lines of psycho-sexual development for a girl: renunciation of sexuality altogether, a 'masculinity complex', or normal femininity where she takes her father as the love object. Translated into literary development these alternatives are: aesthetic frigidity, and the inability to write, as articulated by Rumens; assuming a masculine identity and writing as a man; or identifying herself as feminine. The last way involves a repression of the 'pre-Oedipal' attachment to the mother so that 'we inevitably find women writers oscillating between their matrilineage and their patrilineage in an arduous process of self-definition' (Gilbert and Gubar, 1988: 169), as registered by both Carol Rumens – 'poet or poetess' – and Jane Holland – 'I am a woman and a poet'. As Eavan Boland records, a male-dominated tradition offered her 'War poetry. Nature poetry. Love poetry. Pastoral poetry. The comic epic. The tragic lyric . . . but not the name of my experience, of what I felt and saw' (Boland, 1995: 23) but 'feminism had wonderful strengths as a critique and almost none as an aesthetic' (Boland, 1995: 236). The significance of the Freudian explanation, of course, is that it prescribes women an *essential* ambivalence towards their literary foremothers and that segregation, although necessary to secure equal representation in anthologies, aggravates the affiliation complex. In seeking to replace the negative mythologies of women's poetry with empowering role models we can, however, pursue Gilbert and Gubar's other proposition that Freud's Oedipal stage was invented by men as a reaction formation against the linguistic (as well as the biological) primacy of the mother (Gilbert and Gubar, 1988: 265). Furthermore, the constructed timelessness of the lyric poem provides a means of transcending the oppositional model of male/female traditions; it allows women to evade linearity or historicity and to evoke fantasies which can include the destruction of male dominance and 'the reconstruction of female literary potency' (Gilbert and Gubar, 1988: 210–14). Eavan Boland, for example, discovered a fourth line of artistic development through a specifically female negotiation with poetic traditions (Boland: 1987); this negotiation is a common aesthetic of women's poetry.

Before addressing the way forward, it is important to recognize that the female affiliation complex is evident throughout this century and is persistent. It explains why successful women like Elizabeth Bishop, Kathleen Raine, Laura Riding, and Sheenagh Pugh refuse to be included in women-only anthologies; it explains why Anne Stevenson exclaims, 'to hell with a conglomerate women's tradition' (Stevenson, 1992: 31) and why Carol Ann Duffy hates the term 'woman poet'. The female affiliation complex is discernible over and over again when women write about one another. Linda France, Fleur Adcock and Maura Dooley express regrets at risking 'ghettoising and separatism' (France, 1993: 14) by editing anthologies of women's poetry; in reviewing these anthologies, Elizabeth Lowry, in an essay tellingly titled, 'Relentlessly Feminine: The Flawed Values of *Sixty Women Poets*', condemns Linda France and her poets for 'insisting on an identifiable collective experience' (Lowry 1995: 30–42) and Patricia Craig asks 'Can it *ever* be considered proper to separate the ewes from the sheep? Doesn't this – willy-nilly – suggest that the work in question is being judged by different, possibly less exacting, standards?' (Craig, 1993/4: 59). Rumens, like Lowry and Craig, is clearly antipathetic to women poets collectively in her proposal that there has been enough opening up of the canon and it is time now for 'consolidation, stringency, sifting'; in other words, there are too many women around:

> This book [*Making for Planet Alice: New Women Poets*] would be better if it were leaner. . . . First we had *Sixty Women Poets* (admittedly representing three generations): now, we have thirty poets representing the first half of the '90s.

What will it be next – 2000 Women Poets for the Year 2000? Such profligacy does not benefit women writers: it may in fact ensure that, as far as posterity is concerned, the great and the good will once more, thanks to their gender, be 'hidden from history'.

(Rumens, 1996/7: 26–7)

Carol Rumens, Fleur Adcock, and Anne Stevenson appear to have won acclaim through denying or opposing the perceived femininity or feminist preoccupations which allegedly brought women poets a bad name. However, their unease about being identified by gender has far-reaching implications for the future since it deprives the next generations of positive role models. In contrast, Peter Forbes describes the process of male canon-formation in terms of healthy father–son relations:

> For most of this century there has been a deep collusion between the established generation and the newcomers. There is a clear line from the Movement, through Ian Hamilton's Neo-Movement of the '70s to Blake Morrison, Andrew Motion and Craig Raine in the '80s. The benefits of this system – to everyone but the reader – are obvious. The older generation protect their declining years by having their nominees holding the key jobs and the younger blossom under the benign gaze of the oldies.
>
> (Forbes, 1994: 6)

I am not confident that the senior generations of women are projecting such a benign gaze on the younger ones, particularly since there is little evidence that they are more willing to associate themselves with each other. In the above extract, Peter Forbes was introducing the New Generation Poets of 1994, who consisted of twelve male and eight female poets under 40. When asked to name their influences, three of the women cited only male poets, four cited one or two women plus several men and only one, Sarah Maguire, cited only women, who were all Americans (Adrienne Rich, Elizabeth Bishop and Sylvia Plath). Plath and Bishop were recurring names for the other women as well as for one or two men. Stevie Smith was the only named British woman to be proud of. The sense of writing under the benign gaze of their foremothers is marginally stronger in the women who have emerged since the 1994 promotion, represented by eleven women in the *Poetry Review* (1996/7) special edition of new women poets. These post-New Generation women acknowledged a wider range of female influences, with Plath and Bishop still at the top of the list. In addition, they cited Carol Ann Duffy, Selima Hill, Sharon Olds, Edna St Vincent Millay, Pauline Stainer, Stevie Smith, Denise Riley, Eavan Boland, Vicki Feaver and Wendy Cope. When asked to comment on the 'woman question', nine of the eleven were not interested, not sure or dismissive with statements like: 'I think there are fewer really good poets than people make out, of either gender' (Sophie Hannah); 'I also like a good deal of the poetry coming from men at the moment, which suggests changes of a wider nature than simply issues of gender have taken place' (Gwyneth Lewis) and 'I think a generation of appropriately educated women are reaching an appropriate age' (Kate Clanchy). Only Jane Duran admitted to an awareness of gender politics: 'Women are being heard more, but the balance of power is still with men'. Julia Copus, however, acknowledged the importance of female role models: 'Women poets publishing today are second generation, so to speak. This means not only that the hardest part of the fight has been won for us, but that we have role models where our role models had none' *(Poetry Review, 1996/7: 4–24).* Julia Copus's understanding of the significance of role models sets the agenda for contemporary poets and critics. Her optimism also suggests that the deterministic interpretation of the female affiliation complex can be countered by reading it in terms of patriarchal laws rather than essentialized femininity.

The current way of dealing with the resistance of poets to identification by gender accords with Jan Montefiore's conclusion in 1987, that there is no such thing as 'the woman poet', but

> what does exist is an immense variety of women poets, often divided by major differences of class, race and circumstances, and writing in a multiplicity of discourses, and any account of a woman's tradition has to take account of these differences and separations.

> (Montefiore, 1987: 59)

Editors of anthologies of women's poetry, myself included (Dowson, 1996), tend to claim 'diversity' as the outstanding feature of their contents. This lack of classifiability in terms of gender can seem healthy in a pluralistic postmodern culture and enabling to individual creativity. Some definition must, however, be on the agenda of critics and poets for two reasons: one is that in the absence of any critical framework, however provisional or flexible, the negative myths about women's poetry will persist; the second is that, as Alicia Ostriker observes, to deny that there is such a thing as 'women's poetry', as distinct from poetry by individual women, is only a superficially plausible position, because to say that poetry by women is ungendered is to classify it as male (Ostriker, 1987: 8–9). As Germaine Greer recognizes:

> It suits the male poet to believe that neither sex is specifically intended because it encourages him in his view that his specificity is actually universality. The woman poet who knowingly plays the game is not so much a ventriloquist as a ventriloquist's dummy.

> (Greer, 1995b: 7)

Paradoxically, to argue that women do not all write in the same way is not to say that they do not write as women. Making connections between poets does not limit poetry by women to only one reading position; good poems will be read in terms of gender and also in terms of their cultural contexts and other identities. The point is that while women distance themselves from one another there can be no progress in defining and theorizing women's poetry except negatively in terms of its 'otherness'. As Luce Iragaray puts it, 'symbolising the mother/daughter relationship, creating *externally located* and *durable representations* of this proto-typical relation between women, is an urgent necessity, if women are ever to achieve ontological status in society'.[8]

If, as it appears, women have been distancing themselves from man-made myths about women's poetry as castrated or 'other', the myths need to be exposed and to be supplanted by strong 'mother' figures who relate to a recognizable woman's poetic identity. Although the recovery work of the last twenty years has done much to free nineteenth- and early twentieth-century women from the pejorative stereotypes of femininity, the mythologies surrounding the poetess have been replaced by, or more accurately extended to, mythologies of the woman poet. These offer the contemporary poet a choice between an old-fashioned sentimentalist or the unschooled propagandist. For example, the hoax poet John Whitworth's spoof 'Sonnet', perpetuates the prejudice that women are old-fashioned because they are traditionally formalist:

> Frankly, most Women's Poems are a joke.
> Their sonnets scan. Their rondels rhyme. And worse.
> Their volumes SELL! Of course they cannot hope
> To pass as Poets in the Modern manner.[9]

Although presenting himself as a reconstructed male in his satirical parody of women's poems, Whitworth nevertheless sustains the myth through homogenizing 'Women's Poems'. Women also tend to sustain the myths in their disaffiliations from them; for example, Sarah Maguire echoes Sitwell's aforementioned remarks in her review of *New Virago Poets*: 'Not only does language itself remain flat and unchallenged by the bulk of these writers, but they frequently reiterate the worst stereotypes of femininity, offering intellectually sloppy images of the "eternal feminine"' (Maguire, 1994: 71–2). She does, of course, define herself in opposition to the amateurs in her disparagement of them. In the same review she endorses the other contemporary myth, rooted in the 1960s and 1970s, that feminist critics have over-rated, bad – which means technically slipshod – poetry if it expresses feminist protest:

> And what damages the least successful of these poems so fatally is precisely their authors' failure to appreciate the technical demands of poetry; to grasp that,

without an awareness of structure and form, personal experience remains hermetically personal, and political comment comes over as crass polemic.

(Maguire, 1994: 71–2)

Patricia Craig's review of *Sixty Women Poets* endorses both stereotypes in describing the contents as 'too wrought-up or too wound-down' – and offers women the binary choice of 'the insights of feminism' or 'the essence of femininity' (Craig, 1993/4: 59–60). Fleur Adcock likewise disregards 'the 1960s confessional' in her assertion that women's poetry is not a recognizable genre and Carol Ann Duffy distances herself from the bad connotations of feminism, 'Feminist poetry did play a very useful role in the seventies, but we've moved beyond that' (Duffy, 1990: 61).

Feminist critics need to identify an aesthetic which is broad enough to encompass the variety of poetry by women and which offers them more than one maternal figure. One line of matrilineage this century can be traced from Gertrude Stein to contemporary American language poets like Susan Howe or British experimentalists such as Denise Riley, Wendy Mulford or Veronica Forrest-Thompson (see Mulford, 1990) – interestingly, there are no entries on Riley and Mulford in *The Oxford Companion to Twentieth Century Poetry* (Hamilton, 1994). These poets are bold in their metalinguistic transgressions of traditional poetic boundaries. More often, however, British women negotiate with literary traditions, largely through an appropriation of poetic forms, symbols and cultural references. This appropriation is a solution to the bind between 'John Whitworth's' implication that women's formalism is bad because it is a mere imitation of men's and Sarah Maguire's condemnation of women who fail 'to appreciate the technical demands of poetry'. There is a difference, however, between imitating and appropriating male-associated 'craftsmanship'. For example, in *Sixty Women Poets,* Linda France observed, 'A formal awareness is present even in the work of those poets who apparently eschew tradition' (France, 1993: 19) and in her introduction to *Kicking Daffodils – Twentieth Century Women Poets,* Vicki Bertram suggests that there is a coherence in terms of the ways in which twentieth-century women engage with, question, subvert or recast the mainstreams of British poetry (Bertram, 1997: 2). This is certainly borne out in other current observations: Michael Donaghy identifies the unashamed formalism in Annie Finch's anthology, *A Formal Feeling Comes* (1995) as a breakthrough against the monolith of high modernist criticism (Donaghy, 1995: 69); similarly, Peter Forbes, trying to detect common threads between the eleven newest women poets, concludes, 'There is no dominant style, although the rise of formalism is noteworthy' (Forbes, 1996/7: 3).

I want to dwell on formalism because it has been a problem for women throughout the century and because I detect within feminist criticism a lingering doublespeak concerning the relationship between gender and poetic forms. Edith Sitwell's article, 'Some Observations on Women's Poetry', published in *Vogue* 1925, demonstrates the dilemma for women who could not identify themselves within either feminine or masculine practices:

> Women poets will do best if they realise that male technique is not suitable to them. No woman writing in the English language has ever written a great sonnet, no woman has ever written great blank verse. Then again, speaking generally, as we cannot dispense with our rules, so we find free verse difficult.
> (Sitwell, 1925: 117–18)

Note the association between traditional forms or metres and male technique. As Carol Rumens puts it, women are still left in a no man's land, 'Asking each time I gave birth to a sonnet, / "Is it a boy?" '[10] Gilbert and Gubar were influential in associating forms with repression, because of their man-made origins, whereby a sonnet is perceived as a 'corset'. In contrast, however, in her autobiographical reflections, *Object Lessons: The Life of the Woman and the Poet in Our Time,* Eavan Boland describes her discovery of form as a protective costume, under the cover of which she could develop a poetic self; for her, the elements of form were at first 'part of the costume drama of becoming a poet' (Boland, 1995: 115). Poetic forms need not, therefore, be a suppression of female subjectivity but a strategy for refusing male prescriptions of female subjectivity. For example, women have for a long time impersonated the male voice through dramatic monologue, in a manner currently associated with Carol Ann Duffy, but Anna Wickham, Stevie Smith and Edith Sitwell were doing it at the start of the century. The dramatic monologue puts the male gaze and the male voice, emblems of constructed masculinity, under scrutiny. In their disruptions of traditional metres and displacements of conventional symbols, women can subvert and appropriate the tradition through entry. Sally Minogue's essay, 'Prescriptions and Proscriptions: Feminist Criticism and Contemporary Poetry' is a useful survey of the debate and argues that neither form nor free verse, *per se,* are gendered: 'Poetic forms may have been fashioned largely by men, but this does not render the forms themselves in any way masculine or male; only the association of maleness with poetry does that' (Minogue, 1990: 213). Jan Montefiore also concludes that negotiation with form is, in fact, the place to look for the 'specificity of women's poetry' (Montefiore, 1987: 178–9).

In summary: as we approach the millennium, there is little foundation in literary criticism to believe that women's poetry will accrue an authority which it has failed to do in the last three centuries. Although women publish and win prizes, they are not equally represented in anthologies. There is no consensus about the possibility or desirability of women's poetry as a genre and therefore there are no suitable terms of critical response. In the absence of clear models of self-confessed women poets, myths of the early century poetess and the later century feminist propagandist persist and prevent women from identifying themselves with one another in either the past or the present. Consequently, the older generations do not encourage or promote younger generations in the way that men do and in the way in which canons are formed. The main proposal for the agenda is to make connections between women, whether they are influenced by the American experimentalists, position themselves within oral traditions, participate in the Sapphic continuum of lesbian sexuality or negotiate with British literary traditions. A convincing case can be made that women are able to disrupt poetical norms with an irreverence unencumbered by any nostalgia for a tradition which has ignored them. There is also a developing terminology of other identifiable features which link women across historical and cultural boundaries. Inevitably, many poems are about being a woman and common themes are desire, the search for identity and the right to write; contemporary poets frequently exploit the imaginative possibilities of the lyric which allow them to depict the defeat of patriarchal law through the interface of fantasy and realism. For example, in addition to 'female experience within patriarchy', Linda France identified 'the experience of paradox and the concept of duality and non-linearity', 'the pleasure principle' and 'much laughter, at many pitches . . . irony, parody as well as the big joke' as common features in her sixty poets (France, 1993: 16–17). The rewriting of myths and historical revisionism, which liberate female identity from the stranglehold of nationalism, cultural elitism and chauvinism, are as frequent in women's poems as in their prose.

If anthologies will be used as a register of the contemporary climate, Germaine Greer's statistical analysis of recent anthologies of women poets identifies an unspoken consensus that the major figures are E.J. Scovell, Elma Mitchell, Elizabeth Bartlett, Patricia Beer, Anne Stevenson, U.A. Fanthorpe, Fleur Adcock, Eiléan Ní Chuilleanain, Eavan Boland, Wendy Cope and Selima Hill (Greer, 1995b). Sufficient studies need to be written to support their achievements and studies of all the poets this century need to be written to provide a more representative map. Are there adequate critical works on Maya Angelou, Sujata Bhatt or Jenny Joseph to keep the record straight? Has sufficient attention been paid to poets in the Caribbean or Eastern European traditions, because getting them published is not enough? To keep each other in print, women should cite each other as influences; by acknowledging an affinity with their literary foremothers and sisters they can provide a range of real mother and grand-mother figures for poets to come and the female affiliation complex can be reversed. Literary histories tell us that without adequate literary records, women will be dumped from the stories of this century's poetry and without role models, the myths about 'women's poetry' as a sub-genre will persist. These myths will justify the neglect of literary historians of the future who will be glad to be saved the bother of looking at women's work because it is out of print.

Acknowledgements

Permission to quote from 'A Bookshop Revisited' by Carol Ramens, and 'Strugnell's Incredible Lightness of Being' has been granted by *Poetry Review*.

Permission to quote from 'Pulse' by Jane Holland (from *The Brief History of a Disreputable Woman*, 1997, Bloodaxe) has been granted by Bloodaxe Books.

Notes

Jane Dowson is a Senior Lecturer in English at De Montfort University. Her work on women's poetry includes *Women's Poetry of the 1930s* (Routledge, 1996).

1 Greer is referring to J.C. Squire, who edited *An Anthology of Women's Verse* in 1921.

2 Vita Sackville-West won the Hawthornden Prize in 1924 but her poetry has been out of print for several decades; Ruth Pitter won the Hawthornden Prize in 1937, the Heinemann Award for Literature in 1954 and she was the first woman to receive the Queen's Medal for Poetry in 1959, but she is not well known.

3 Edith Sitwell, Letter to Stephen Spender, 16 March 1946 (Lehmann and Parker, 1970: 136–7).

4 Edith Sitwell, letter to Maurice Bowra, Jan. 24, 1944 (Lehmann and Parker, 1970: 116).

5 Amy Lowell, 'The Sisters', from *What's O'Clock* (1925), *Complete Poetical Works* (1955: 459–61).

6 Jane Holland, from 'Pulse' (Dooley, 1997: 97).

7 Carol Rumens, from 'A Bookshop Revisited', *Poetry Review*, Vol. 86 (4) (1996/7: 36–7).

8 Luce Iragaray, cited in Yorke (1991: 183). Liz Yorke is discussing representations of the lesbian body and lesbian bonding, but her point about creating new paradigms of the mother/daughter relationship in order to overcome the female affiliation complex can also apply to the wider community of women poets.

9 John Whitworth, 'Strugnell's Incredible Lightness of Being', *Poetry Review*, Winter (1996/7: 77).

10 Carol Rumens, from 'A Bookshop Revisited', *Poetry Review* (1996/7: 36–7).

References

ADCOCK, Fleur (1987) editor, *The Faber Book of Twentieth Century Women's Poetry*, London: Faber.

BERTRAM, Vicki (1997) editor, *Kicking Daffodils – Twentieth Century Women Poets*, Edinburgh: Edinburgh University Press.

BOLAND, Eavan (1987) 'The woman poet: her dilemma' *American Poetry Review*, Vol. 16, Jan./Feb., pp. 17–20.

—— (1995) *Object Lessons: The Life of the Woman and the Poet in Our Time*, Manchester: Carcanet.

CLARK, Suzanne (1991) *Sentimental Modernism: Women Writers and the Revolution of the Word*, Bloomington and Indianapolis: Indiana University Press.

CRAIG, Patricia (1993/4) 'Redressing the balance' review of **FRANCE** (1993) in *Poetry Review*, Vol. 83, No. 4, Winter, pp. 59–60.

DONAGHY, Michael (1995) 'A defence of breathing', review of **Annie Finch** (1995) editor, *A Formal Feeling Comes*, Story Line Press in *Poetry Review*, Vol. 85, No. 1, Spring, pp. 69–70.

DOOLEY, Maura (1997) editor, *Making for Planet Alice: New Women Poets*, Newcastle upon Tyne: Bloodaxe.

DOWSON, Jane (1996) editor, *Women's Poetry of the 1930s*, London: Routledge.

DUFFY, Carol Ann (1990) Interview in *Options*, June, p. 61.

FORBES, Peter (1994) 'Talking about the new generation', *Poetry Review*, Vol. 84, No. 1, Spring, pp. 4–6.

—— (1996/7) 'Beyond the bell jar', *Poetry Review*, Vol. 86, No. 4, Winter, p. 3.

FRANCE, Linda (1993) editor, *Sixty Women Poets*, Newcastle upon Tyne: Bloodaxe.

GILBERT, Sandra and GUBAR, Susan (1988) *No Man's Land: The Place Of The Woman Writer In The Twentieth Century*. Vol. 1. *The War Of The Words*, New Haven and London: Yale University Press.

GREER, Germaine (1995a) *Slipshod Sibyls: Recognition, Rejection and the Woman Poet*, New York: Viking Press.

—— (1995b) 'A biodegradable art: changing fashions in anthologies of women's poetry', *Times Literary Supplement*, 30 June, pp. 7–8.

HAMILTON, Ian (1994) editor, *The Oxford Companion to Twentieth Century Poetry*, Oxford: Blackwell.

HEANEY, Seamus and HUGHES, Ted (1997) editors, *The School Bag*, London: Faber.

LEHMANN, John and PARKER, Derek (1970) editors, *Edith Sitwell: Selected Letters*, London: Macmillan.

LOWELL, Amy (1955) *Complete Poetical Works*, Boston: Houghton Mifflin Company.

LOWRY, Elizabeth (1995) 'Relentlessly feminine: the flawed values of *Sixty Women Poets*' *Thumbscrew*, No. 2, Spring, pp. 30–42.

MAGUIRE, Sarah (1994) 'The craftsperson's contract', review of SILGARDO and BECK (1993) *New Virago Poets, Poetry Review*, pp. 71–2.

MILNE, W.S. (1995) review of Carol Ann Duffy (1994) *Selected Poems* (Harmondsworth: Penguin) *Outposts*, 180/181, Spring/Summer pp. 157–8.

MINOGUE, Sally (1990) 'Prescriptions and proscriptions: feminist criticism and contemporary poetry' in Sally Minogue (1990) editor, *Problems for Feminist Criticism*, London: Routledge.

MONTEFIORE, Jan (1987) *Feminism and Poetry: Language, Experience, Identity in Women's Writing*, London: Pandora.

MULFORD, Wendy (1990) ' "Curved, odd . . . irregular". A vision of contemporary poetry by women' *Women: A Cultural Review*, Vol. 1, Winter, pp. 261–74.

OSTRIKER, Alicia (1987) *Stealing the Language: The Emergence of Women's Poetry in America*, London: Women's Press.

Poetry Review (1994) Special edition on the New Generation Poets, Vol. 84, No. 1, Spring.

—— (1996/7) Special edition on new women poets, Vol. 86, No. 4, Winter.

RUMENS, Carol (1996/7) 'My leaky coracle', review of DOOLEY (1997) *Poetry Review*, Vol. 86, No. 4, Winter, pp. 26–7.

SANSOM, Ian (1995) 'Wayne's world', review of Carol Ann Duffy (1994) *Selected Poems* (Harmondsworth: Penguin) *London Review of Books*, 6 July, p. 20.

SILGARDO, Melanie and BECK, Janet (1993) editors, *New Virago Poets*, London: Virago.

SITWELL, Edith (1925) 'Some observations on Women's Poetry' *Vogue*, Vol. 65, No. 5, March, pp. 117–18.

SQUIRE, J.C. (1921) editor, *An Anthology of Women's Verse*, Oxford: Clarendon Press.

STEVENSON, Anne (1992) 'Some notes on women and tradition' *PN Review*, No. 87, Vol. 19, Sept./Oct., pp. 29–32.

YORKE, Liz (1991) *Impertinent Voices: Subversive Strategies in Contemporary Women's Poetry*, London: Routledge.

In Case of Emergency Break Glass

Helen Kidd

FEMINIST REVIEW NO 62, SUMMER 1999, ISSN 0141-7789, PP. 21–23

The ghosts of trees
an underwater sun
sanderlings skimming
windows' blinkers
or a glimpse in a mirror
sister.

Sitting in apple galleons' tops
or watching rain curtains
sluice the skylight
in the shed, with plum stones,
cores and mouse droppings
we pored over old *Eagles*.
I liked Dan Dare. You laughed
at Harris Tweed. The Mekon
lived next door.

You were the queen
of scrumping. You could
jump from high up the stairs
catch the pole, swing like Flynn
into the hall. You taught me how
to hang by the backs of my knees
from big branched trees
to find the best conkers
in the graveyard rich-seamed
and toe-nailed in spiny cradles.
You and me kicking up yellow
shoals in the autumn
in the fronds of half-light.

Algebra, uniforms, the Latin
enigma and girls in grey
swimming the corridors . . .
when did you leave?
There was you and me
and our blue bike
our hot water-bottle
our red scarf, our torn duffel
but when I wasn't looking
you went up to the burn
and then dwindled . . .

The nagging space of
a pulled tooth
the knot in the hanky
that didn't work
and the windows all open
to shadows
like sour milk
and soot fall.

(The man in the mack got lucky).
What was the spell
to hold off the dark?
A something. . . ?

Searching where it glimmed
at the edge of the mirror
a space nibbling
the edge of my thinking.
The sound of a room
just empty. The footprint
collecting the rain
The dent in the pillow.

Then the sudden
shimmer of air reshaping

and you
        vaulting the sill
of memory . . . my Lone Ranger
sister defeating the shufflers
with *Leave her alone!*

Just leave her alone
you bastards!
with breast-plate and spear
with cutlass and dagger.
Until you rode off
over the tall hill
on our blue bike
taking our red scarf
our torn duffel
and I banged the old gate
that creaked in the night wind
behind me forever.

But the pressure of light
to a glim at the edge
of the mirror is her spark
in my eye. Her laugh
in my mouth. Her grin
on the bright ghost
of a face still swims
like a fish through the trees
writing my life in windows.

Note

Helen Kidd is a poet, reviewer and co-editor of *The Virago Book of Love Poetry* (1990). Her latest work is *Origami* (Maquette Press, Devon, 1999) and *Sleight of Foot* (Reality Street Four Pack, 1996). She lectures in English Studies at Oxford Brookes University, and also works with Participatory Arts Projects in hospices and MIND centres. She writes for *Poetry Quarterly Review* and has published a number of essays on contemporary poetry, most recently for *Kicking Daffodils: Twentieth Century Women Poets*, ed. Vicki Bertram. (Edinburgh University Press, 1997).

A Round-Table Discussion on Poetry in Performance

Jean Binta Breeze, Patience Agbabi, Jillian Tipene, Ruth Harrison and Vicki Bertram

FEMINIST REVIEW NO 62, SUMMER 1999, ISSN 0141-7789, PP. 24–54

Keywords

poetry in performance; performance poets; women poets on stage; Black women poets; Black British; Arts Council/Board funding; politics and poetry

Ruth Harrison (RH): Can we start with economics? It's the most important bit, isn't it? So, let's start by looking at your sources of income and how you get your work – or how you'd like to get your work – and what sort of pressures are on you, as a woman poet, in making your living that way.

Jean Breeze (JB): Well, I've been freelancing since 1987, but I survive because I do so many different things. So there's the occasional acting job, occasional stuff in television, and I've written two full-length screen plays. And so I get writing jobs. But the basis of my income is, actually, performance. The returns on my books could probably keep me in cigarettes! Because it takes a long time before you start getting royalties from publications. So the basis of my income has been performance.

Vicki Bertram (VB): What about the records, and other recordings: do you get anything from those?

JB: No. No. No, I mean, a lot of street cred!

RH: So it's performance and workshops, really, which are the back-bone of your income?

JB: Yeah. And writing. Certainly writing for film and TV.

RH: What about you, Patience?

Patience Agbabi (PA): Well, I'd say performance is the majority of my income and, I suppose, workshops as well, mainly with kids, 15-year-olds, Year Ten. Everyone wants Year Ten to learn about poetry. So workshops, and Housing Benefit. I've been on Housing Benefit since I've been in this business. I haven't managed to get off it.

Patience Agbabi

Jillian Tipene (© Kim Fielding)

Jean 'Binta' Breeze

VB: Do you also do other work, though?

PA: I do. I have worked in a medical publishing company on and off in the past few years, but I've actually given that up, because I was finding I wasn't creating anything new. I was just working and working and working and still, somehow, wasn't managing to move forwards, so I decided that I'd have to give up that work, which meant I had less money, but I have actually been writing. So it's a sacrifice I thought I'd have to make, because the economic side is important, but the spiritual, creative side is important too, and trying to keep that balance is difficult, it's a very delicate balance.

VB: Do you have an agent?

PA: No, I don't.

VB: Is that because it would be impossible to find one, or you don't want one?

PA: I'd love to have an agent. I spend about 20 per cent of the time doing business and admin., and a lot of the admin. just doesn't get done, like filing, it just does not get done, quite literally, it just piles up, and . . . I think one of the problems is, unless you're very, very well known as a performance poet, you're not earning enough to really tempt an agent. You know, I do think there's an issue with that. I did have an agent last year; it didn't work out. She claimed she was on 50p an hour! So . . . yeah . . . it is kind of hard, in the sense of tempting agents, unless you're earning a substantial amount.

RH: But there are very few agents who actually work within performance poetry anyway. I mean, you're potentially looking at a music agent, rather than a literary agent. That's what most poets would have if they're page-based – a literary agent. There's an issue about how economically viable it is for an agent to even have performance poets on their books because, given the fees and the percentages an agent would take, you'd have to be getting a lot of work, or be commanding quite a large fee to make it actually worthwhile for the agent to be doing it.

PA: Yeah. I mean, I think if an agent were working with performance poets, I'd like to see, say, somebody decide to take on three women, or certainly take on more than one.

Jillian Tipene (JT): But also market them, in creative ways. This is gonna come up several times in this conversation, but, you know, the breakthrough has been made by none other than Murray Laughlan Young, and, you know, why aren't poets doing ads on TV, for Virgin First Class, never mind Economy [Virgin Airline company]? And, why isn't it one of us? But I think that there is a slow, a pin-hole opening, and if agents could be more aware . . . of course, you know, they don't wanna do the donkey work, but if they could become aware that there are ways to market poets in the climate that exists now, into more lucrative avenues, then things might start to open up. But I think it also involves poets themselves beginning to show that they can be utilized in that way.

JB: I've always had a kind of defence system, though, against being marketed, because I'd say most of my work has been built over many many years. I came here in 1985, and prior to that, for about eight years, I was actually performing in Jamaica, and now it's, what, twelve years here . . . I get a lot of re-bookings, and I couldn't possibly exist without Paul Beasley. And Paul and I have been working very closely together for the twelve years that I have been in the country, when he was pretty much my agent informally, and I had to, at one stage, say, 'Paul, come on! This is a job you're doing! Let's deal with it!' And so for about eight years, he's been officially acting as my agent. And because he had such a grounding in the development of poetry in this country, from his early days with Apples & Snakes, who were one of the only groups to actually book new poets coming in, and new voices, so he had all that experience. So, between him having really good contacts throughout Britain, you know, for venues and festivals and so on, and just having done years of it, so that people know what they're getting and why they wanna book you, . . . and also because I'm an extremely lazy person, so I couldn't . . . I mean, I taught for seven years, full-time, in Jamaica and here, and I couldn't really think of making the day job. So I'd rather have less money and live the lifestyle that I actually lead. I'm not an extravagant person, I need very little ... do you see what I'm saying? I like the time that I have for myself. I'm not a disciplined writer, I have no hours of writing or anything, but I do like time to just sit still.

VB: But, as you say, you've built up connections and a name, so maybe you don't need the marketing. What Jillian was saying seemed very interesting, in terms of how you might get in there, if you're not already in there? Poets on adverts, for example.

JB: But then you'd have to think about what you're advertising; the politics of advertising is just so dodgy . . . I mean, I did a performance in Zurich on the night when Nelson Mandela actually walked out of Robben Island. It was an incredible moment on stage, a huge concert in Zurich, with Lynton Kwesi Johnson. Then afterwards, when the press were interviewing me, they asked, how did I feel about being sponsored for the show by a tobacco company that had all kinds of problems with its workers in a Third World country? Which I hadn't even known, when I entered the game. So I'm always, like, really really wary of anything like that, because the politics that you're talking about can be so completely undermined by companies. . .

JT: I was very struck when Patience told me how she made the decision one day, that she was going to be a poet, and I was thinking about that, this morning. You know, that crystal moment when you think, 'Okay, I'm taking a leap. I'm going to make my living as a poet'. But then, why should that necessarily have to mean that you surrender yourself to a life of tatters and making do, you know? I mean, why should the whole image of being a poet have to mean a kind of a half-arsed existence? And I am asking myself that question, and I'm just saying that maybe it's possible to see being a poet as a lucrative business, if you wanna go to that realm.

RH: I don't know which edition of *Poetry Review* it's in, but in the Editorial Peter Forbes says one of the reasons why performance poetry is never really going to get acknowledged is because it doesn't have copyright, basically, because that's the traditional way of poets earning money through their books, and a way that you can then authenticate the work, because it's on the page. Of course, performance poetry is about the stage, it is about getting up there, and that can't be reproduced: you're paid your fee, but then after that, there's nothing. So he's saying that it's transient, and of the moment, which is all, I'd say, very positive. But he's saying that's an inhibitor for it actually to progress into something which could then earn poets money. But obviously, it is earning poets money, because you're getting fees for it. But he was using that as a kind of derogatory thing, saying that this kind of work has not overcome the problem of actually being reproduced in some way.

PA: There is something about longevity, though. I mean, I got to a stage in '95, where my book was coming out, and it's very important to have a book, it's very important to have something concrete and solid. I'd been working since 1990, so that was six years. And I remember being aware that all the performance poets who I thought had made it, had all got books, and I thought that wasn't a coincidence. I mean, a lot of them had been on LPs and so on as well, but I thought to be published was really important. And since '95, my career has been steadily building, you know, very very slowly, but it has taken a much more upward curve since the book, because so many people see it, and have heard of you. So when my agent was proactively phoning somebody, and they had actually heard of me, then it made a big difference.

VB: There is also this distinction between performance poetry and page poetry which seems to me very difficult. I mean, if you hear Carol Ann Duffy reading and then you go away and read her work printed, you can still hear her voice, and that is crucial. There's almost nothing like hearing a poet read their work, or perform their work, and so the distinction is . . . I mean, I know it's taking us off economics a bit, but I wonder whether it's a distinction you, you are happy with? Are you happy to be called 'performance poets'?

JB: I was published because the publishers realized that I had an audience that would buy the books; I wasn't published and then developed an audience, I was published because the publishers realized that there was some money to be made.

RH: Well, it's interesting. I mean, you might have been published because of that, through Bloodaxe or whatever, but a lot of the poets published by someone like Bloodaxe don't already have an audience. They are published because of their artistic merit, so it raises questions like, why are you published by someone like Bloodaxe? I think there are other things going on there, really, because if a white woman poet approaches Bloodaxe, and they think it's artistic, then they will publish regardless of whether that person has got an audience or has ever even gone out there and done a

performance.

JB: Well, that's not what happened with Bloodaxe, because Bloodaxe have done my fourth book, you know. I'm talking, like, in the early days, when I was first published. I mean, with Bloodaxe, it's the way I like things to happen. I went and did a reading, and one of the partners was there, and simply said, 'Do you have a manuscript?' But in the early days, I mean, there was no thought of publishing my work, because the question asked by my first and my second publishers in this country, was 'Will it work on the page?' But because there were 2,000 people in Camden Centre giving me a standing ovation, obviously, it's worth putting it on the page, you see.

PA: Yes, I had that happen a lot, in '93, '94: people saying, 'Well, are you published?' And then, 'Why aren't you published? You should be published.' I had got to the stage of thinking, 'I'm a performance poet'. I had originally sent poems out to people, and had been published in one or two places, like *Feminist Review*, and then I started building my performance career, and just stopped sending things out, not because I thought they wouldn't be published, but because I was focusing on that side of my career. And then it came to a stage where there were certain poems which were so popular that people were coming up to me with money . . . I didn't have a book, and that was painful. And so, since then, the book's sold pretty well, so it does work on the page. Some of the more popular poems are more accessible. I think they're well written, but they're not the sort of poems that you'd sit down for five hours and dissect. They're more immediate than that.

JB: Well, to me, there's something called poetry, and it exists in language, in any language, any person speaking: a fisherman on the beach, or a man in the pub, you know, a woman washing can be speaking poetry, but they haven't necessarily written a poem. I think that is a kind of development. So poetry, for me, exists outside of form, you know, so the whole . . . it's almost a conceit, in a way, to say, 'Here is a poem', because it's simply about language, and how language is used through metaphor and . . . and people do it all the time in their daily lives. So to really say 'I'm a poet' creates all kinds of difficulties, because are you all the time . . . you know, using language well? Do you see what I'm saying? So I look at poetry as something that you recognize wherever it crops up. So I have no difficulties between page or stage. Poetry is something that you recognize as a way of using language well, and it crops up everywhere that people use language. I'm not saying that everybody wants to go and write it down, right? But poetry is not about whether it's written down, or whether it's on the stage. It's about a particular way of using language.

VB: But while that's the case, the economics of it, in terms of being published, and selling your books, do carry a lot of weight, don't they? I mean, as Patience was saying, it was through having the book published, she became better known.

PA: Definitely.

JT: It depends. I mean, look at Akure Wall: her essence is in the oral, the oral aspect of her work, so she makes a CD. And for some people, that makes a lot more sense than publishing a book. Well, she did self-publish one of her little books. . .

RH: But, actually, it's interesting what she did with the CD as well: within it, there was a book, because all the poems were actually within that.

PA: Yeah, there's quite a lot of rap albums where they do that anyway. That's where poetry crosses over into lyrics and the music scene.

JT: You know, what it really comes down to is, who defines what poetry is? And how much do we let that affect where we take our work?

RH: But I think it's not only how you define your work, it's also what access you actually have to get your work out, because my perception of the way the poetry system works over here is that there is a divide between the page and the stage, and that there are people within the established poetry network, who don't approve of performance poetry, who don't approve of people going out there on the stage. They don't see that as poetry, and they don't think it's worthy of being published. And that does inhibit the progress of certain types of poetry, because I think it would be very difficult for certain types of poets, in this country, to get published, and being published is actually seen as the main critical thing, to say that you are more of an established poet. I think that works against a lot of poets who are coming from an oral tradition.

JB: Well, you see, to me, all the art forms are interlinked, and poetry on the page, to me, is a link with the visual arts, in terms of how the book looks, how the poems are put on the page, all that stuff, it links itself to the visual arts. Poetry on the stage links itself to the performing arts, and each individual working with language has a tendency, or a stronger tendency, to one or the other. So there are poets who like to see the book, and they know exactly how they want it designed, they know how the poem must look on the page and, you know, whether they want illustrations or not. All kinds of visual things that they want about the book. Right? And there are poets who know exactly how they want it to sound, what they want to do with their bodies on the stage, and their strength is towards that. And I think it's a largely individual thing. So I'm saying that, yes, there might be established ideas about what makes you seem to be a more serious poet: it might be to have a book and all of that, but we can't play to what it seems to other folks, because then you're constantly in reaction to something that is outside of your control. What I'm about is, what are your individual strengths? What is it that your poem demands of you? And you give the poem that. Because I don't think any poet, in this country, earns as much as Lynton Kwesi Johnson does, and he has taken his poetry all the way on stage, and into albums. Yes, people put out copies of his books, but it's his albums that sell, and he's playing to huge, huge crowds, as a poet, by going to the music, instead of to the visual arts, or the book, or even to the more kind of theatre arts that I go towards. He's gone directly to music, and there are these avenues open . . . Poets like him are not found via publishing at all, and it has not affected their economics! In fact, they're making much more, because you make more as a live act on the stage, than you do from the returns for a book.

RH: This raises a question around what sort of criticism, or what kind of critical levels you want for your work. How important is it to have a literary critique of your work? In this country, it has got to be book-based, because there is no critical language for performance-based critique . . .

JB: Well, Lynton is getting his critique through music magazines much more. He gets academic critique now, because he's been there for so long. So, you know, he's got more reviews coming in than we have.

RH: But what about you though . . . as women poets, where do you get your critical feedback, and what sort of critical feedback do you actually want? Do you want it from academic journals? Do you want to see a review of your work in the *Guardian*, what sort of feedback do you require?

JB: Well, I find that people don't often critique the work. Everybody wants interviews with you about your personal life! And, you know, I get a lot of press, and they all ask the same questions, usually. And it's about my personal life, and how I write, and my children. But nobody ever takes the work and says, 'I'm going to critique the work', or come to a performance, and critique the performance, like how you critique a play.

JT: They don't really know what they're doing, do they?

JB: And the best criticism that I've had on the page, you know, academic, has been from the people in the West Indies, in particular, writing on Caribbean poetry, and critiquing it in ways that were very helpful to me, because I then saw the links, I then saw the resonance of a tradition of which I was a part, and really wonderful things about the women, and how they linked . . . the women I was writing, how they linked with women in Caribbean myth. And it was really interesting . . . but that was coming out of the University of West Indies.

31

RH: Yeah, not from here.

JB: Who understand where I'm coming from.

VB: Is that the same for you, Patience?

PA: Well, I'd love to be given an in-depth critique in the *Guardian*, a full page, that would be great! There's a couple of things: one of them was a paper given by Anita Naoko Pilgrim, at 'Kicking Daffodils II' [women and poetry conference / festival, held at Oxford Brookes University in 1994 and 1997], about one of my poems, which was absolutely amazing, because it was so detailed and so academic, and it was wonderful. And I actually understood it as well! And that's the sort of criticism that I, personally, would like to have. I recognize not all my poems will undergo that type of criticism, but at least half of them would, and certainly, the next book I'm writing, definitely would.

VB: Why do you want that? I mean, is it because it's interesting to see people reading things, finding things that you didn't see in it? Or is it because she points out weaknesses, or strengths?

PA: Well, it's because a lot of thought's gone into them.

VB: Right, so you felt that you'd got a really attentive reader.

PA: Well, you want your poetic skills to be acknowledged; you want to be recognized for having a brain in your head.

JB: What it did for me was that I didn't feel lonely. And one of the wonderful things about going to writers' conferences and listening to people critique stuff, is that you understand that there are so many women out there doing the same thing, and to have a sense of where a character you've written comes from, in a Haitian rhythm, whether they come from Jamaica or . . . and you just don't feel lonely.

JT: I do feel that I'd appreciate a lot more criticism from some of my peers, and I think that, on the whole, on the scene, there is no critiquing of each other's work, in a positive way, . . . there's lots of criticism, maybe, behind the back, and it's not always very generous.

RH: Well, it's usually not about the poetry!

JT: Well, it can be, but it's not 'how can we support that person and help them grow?' And I think that a kind of a level, a standard on the performance circuit would help, because it's so diverse, you know. But if there's a standard and a certain level of . . . I don't know what to call it, but where it can be open to being . . . not judged, but critiqued by literary people, why not?

VB: If Patience goes to one of your performances, do you then talk about it? Or are there other poets you talk with? Or do you each feel, 'Well, this is private', you know, or 'I can't judge'? I mean, is there also something about 'am I the right person to judge? Do I have the expertise?'

JT: Well, it's more about caring about that person, I guess. It ties into one of these other questions, which is about peer group, and I think that I, personally, have a group, I'm lucky to have a peer group of people that I respect, and follow their work, and follow their progress, and will go to see, and I would like to think that there is an openness to exchanging criticism of each other's work. It tends to be a lot more . . . 'Great', you know, 'Oh, I loved it. Loved it! Great!' And we're all very congratulatory of each other, and I hope that's because . . . that's what they felt, as opposed to, 'Well, they're my friend, and I can't tell them I hated it.'

JB: I was very lucky in the early years, I had really really good people around me, wonderful poets that I respected. I used to take my poems to Mervyn Morris, in the early days, and Dennis Scott, who are both tremendous poets, Jamaican poets, and who were actually . . . you know, I was a student at the time, and they were there, already established, and, . . . I used to take my poems to them. Nowadays, I send stuff to Carolyn Cooper. But the wonderful thing about the way they treated me was that they never interfered with my voice. They never interfered. I can say that now. And so I don't have such a need for the criticism as I might have done without them, because of what they allowed me, and I don't quite know how they did it, except that their personal politics must be really right on! And they have no power problems, because people can be very dangerous if they are into power, when they're getting into your work. And some people, like, wanna recreate themselves in you, and all of that, and I was very fortunate that that didn't happen to me. And now, I have a really strong sense of my own voice, as a woman, because I write a lot of voices; more than introspective stuff, I write voices, and I have a sense of the truth of those voices, and I know, during the writing, the truth of that voice. I don't edit at all, because I live with it for a long time in my head, and the writing only takes fifteen minutes, because I've lived with it for the last year or something, five years or whatever, in my head, that voice. So when that voice comes through, I only have to be true to that voice. So I'm not looking out for authenticity, I look inside for authenticity.

VB: But that's really interesting, because you were saying you started out working in Jamaica, and you had these supportive people, but . . . Patience and Jillian, are you finding people who can assess your work for you, who understand the traditions that it's coming out of?

PA: Yeah. Afro-style School is this group that's led by Kwame Dawes who comes over about twice a year, and it's all young black poets who attend – Jillian was on the most recent one – and, basically, there's a set of about ten of us. It's mainly women, interestingly; it's mixed, but it's mainly women, about eight women and two men. And I found that that, for me, has been the most helpful process of criticism. I mean, Kwame Dawes scrutinizes in quite an academic way, but I really like that, I feel I need that, because I need to be kept on my toes. But, at the same time, he himself has written books about reggae, and he performs, and he also reads, so he has an understanding. It's not as if he's like, 'Oh, well, that's performance poetry, I don't wanna deal with that'. He has an understanding of where I'm coming from, so that, for me, has been really helpful, and that's been the past two years. And I'm also in Atomic Lip, which is a very performance-based group, but we actually critique each other's poems, line by line, you know. We've only just started doing that, but we started because we had that need. I've just written a poem a hundred lines long; it's taken me about a year to write it, and Steve actually went through and marked it, and gave it back. There were very few red marks, but everything he said, I completely agreed with. I'm really really pleased I did that. So I need that still. I mean, I've been writing for over ten years, and I still need that support. Without that, I'd find it very difficult to carry on.

JT: I went to see Alice Walker the other night, she said, 'Don't give your heart to someone who eats hearts', and I think it's really crucial that you're giving your work to be critiqued to someone who you respect, and who you know supports who you are, and is interested in you thriving. I feel very grateful, being here, that I do have in Kwame and a few other people, avenues of support, and really valid and relevant feedback.

PA: Another brilliant thing I've been doing recently is performing to undergraduates, doing a so-called lecture. I've recently worked at Roehampton Institute, where I do a half-hour performance, and a half-hour Question and Answer session, and that's very helpful to me as a writer, because they're all studying English, so they've got this way of asking questions. I do sessions in schools too, but when they're undergrads, they ask intelligent questions, and it's good for you to be asked 'who is your audience?' and be forced to think, 'yeah, who is my audience?' That's really important, because sometimes I can just write and perform, and write and perform, and do workshops and I can be incredibly busy, which is great, actually, but sometimes you don't have that time to step back and evaluate, so it's good doing gigs like that. When you do standard evening gigs, people might come up and say, 'It's great'. I want them to say, 'I like that poem *because* . . .' and occasionally you'll get that. Occasionally you'll get someone who'll quote your words back at you, and it's, like, 'Wow! Let's sit down in the corner and have a chin-wag.'

RH: Who do you perceive your audience to be, really? Or do you even have a conception of who your audience is . . . of an audience with whom you feel safe?

JT: I had an experience, very recently, that shocked the pants off me! And that was going to Poole, and teaching a workshop to a group of branch librarians. I thought I was safe, it was a group of women, fourteen women. I thought I'd perform my signature poem for them, which is a beautiful journey called 'Blue'. It gets nothing but raves, so I performed for them while they were drinking their coffee and their biscuits, and then I sat down and asked them to please introduce themselves, and tell me a bit about how they felt about poetry. The hostility that came at me, I was gob-smacked! But secure enough to see it as . . . as their fear, their complete . . . you know, the way I'd invaded their nice secure existence. 'We like traditional poetry.' And, 'We don't know what on earth you're doing'. And, 'Do you deliberately set out to shock people, by using words such as "vulva" and "amniotic" and "umbilical"?' I was, like, 'What?!' So it was, oh, take the pink sun-glasses off: outside London there is complete incomprehension of what I'm doing! So maybe my audience is 'multi-cultural', or at least aware of a multi-cultural existence. I feel very comfortable with a black audience, and with a female audience in general . . . I'm learning that it's really important that you don't underestimate an audience, you don't judge an audience, right off the bat, because I've walked into places where I've thought, 'I'm gonna sink like a stone', and been very pleasantly surprised. I've walked into places where I've thought, 'Yeah! I'm home!' And not a tinkle! So maybe it's as universal as Jean said: that everything is poetry, and we are here to communicate to everybody, and some people will be receptive and some people won't.

JB: I'm theatre-trained, and I've been a teacher for many many years, and I have a really genuine desire, anywhere that I go, to begin a conversation. So for me, there are certain venues that require performance. Space has a lot to do with it, as well as the people who come into that conversation with you. Many times the space decides the format of the performance. So, obviously, if you end up in a theatre with people seated quite formally, and you're on an elevated stage, there are things you can do, which you can't do if you end up in a library, or if you're in a community centre somewhere, or if you're on a reggae stage. They are completely different things. And what I think I have is an awareness of space. I never actually plan a performance. I wait to get into the space, and for the conversation, to see who I am with, who am I talking to? And in that sense, I am multi-lingual. I only speak Jamaican and English, but in a sense, I am multi-lingual in terms of people's experiences. And people always ask me, what are your themes? What do you write about? But I write about everything, just about everything. So I always wait and find what the conversation is, and then begin. And also, there are levels to a performance, particularly where you pitch your voice . . . there's all kinds of elements to performance that have nothing to do with writing, except that I write for it! Where you pitch your voice at certain kinds of people, the choice of the material, what conversation you start. . . Part of what I love about performance is kind of . . . melting in a situation, and training my voice over the years, as a seducer to listening. And I'm not much into shock tactics, I'm kind of, like, you know, 'Well, let's get a little bit of love going here first', and then I will gradually say, 'Well, maybe we need to look at this'. Or something like that. But that's how I am as a person, you know, I just carry me, and it's like . . . you walk into any room, and you know immediately what the vibes are, and what you're dealing with, and so on, and I don't think that comes from writing training, I think that comes because of my own personal history and what I have done with my life over the years, and that makes it easy to do. And I really like kind of melting things down.

RH: Have you ever failed to melt the audience down?

JB: Schools: I was put into a room, a classroom of 10-year-old boys once, and I realized that to go in there and read my poems, was like, not what was happening. So instead of doing a performance of my poems, I got all the boys to write football songs, because I don't see the point in beating my head against a brick wall. I will pull other skills, and still make it happen. Something, at least to do with language. I don't have any kind of sense of myself as . . . *this is Jean Binta Breeze*, and when you book me, this is what you get!' I don't do it, because, like I say, I just melt! I just melt into whatever is going down.

VB: So what you're offering is a highly skilful performance, isn't it, in that you're adapting yourself to suit . . . whereas the traditional poet will turn up and will expect people to listen in the way that the poet wants to be listened to.

JB: I don't maintain any kind of purisms about it. I love language, and I love meeting people, and I love finding out where their conversation is at, and I join that conversation, because I think it awfully rude if people are having a conversation and somebody comes in and just . . . always is, like, going across. Unless it's funny! You think of that as rude at a dinner party. So why should you do that to people who have gathered in your name?

RH: What about you, Patience?

PA: My audience? I think it's mainly women. It's not exclusively women, but in terms of who buys my books at gigs, about 70 per cent women. People occasionally send me fan mail! Yeah, very occasionally I get stuff, and it's always from women. When I was writing, I was, in a sense, writing for a general audience, but I knew women would get it more. I just knew women would relate, in that sense. So I suppose it's no surprise. But certainly with the stuff from *R.A.W.*, it tends to be more women – lesbian and straight. I do have some male fans too, and also a general black audience is always going to respond more, and understand more. But Black women are my number one fans. I've done quite a lot of workshops for women as well, you know, women-only workshops, which I really really enjoy doing.

VB: And when you write the poems, do you have a listener in mind? I mean, I guess it will depend on the poem, but is there any way in which you can generalize and say, ' I'm addressing my imaginary listener'?

JT: I don't.

PA: Myself! Usually, it's me. If I write stuff, it's the sort of stuff I want to read.

JT: For me, it's more an impulse. It's an impulse to write a work, a work that wants to, that needs to come, and then afterwards I'll look at it, and ask, 'What is this? Where does it go?' But it's an impulse, I don't intellectualize, or think of where it might go.

JB: I think my commitment is to the voice that I am writing, and to write that as it is. It will then decide who it speaks to. On the other hand, there are certain performances that I have, when I know who my audience is going to be, and I know them so well that I know where the conversation is at. And if I don't have something that addresses that conversation, I will write particularly for that performance. Like the Sisters' Celebration: I know these are all black women, and I know I have an hour; say, I'm doing one poem at a benefit gig, for black sisters, for Women's Day. And I know what the audience is going to be, I know that they've come out to have a good evening, with lots of comedians on, and I think, 'Well, what's the conversation that's happening? What can I add to this conversation?' And I'll write something for it.

PA: Yeah. That's a really good point. I've also written poems for particular events. I did a Justice for Women benefit, for Kiranjit Ahluwalia several years ago, and I wrote *Sentences* for that. Of course, I've performed it a lot since then, but that's what I wrote the poem for, specifically. And I wrote 'The Black, The White and The Blue', for a Newham Monitoring Project benefit. And it's interesting, I think some of my best pieces come from that experience, because there's an intensity of both political issue and absolute deadline.

JT: Well it's about form as well isn't it? When you impose form, it creates a tension, and sometimes when you're asked to write something, I find, it's quite difficult, and you strain a little bit, and it pushes you into areas that you wouldn't normally go. And then, later, you look at it, and you think, 'Well!' Because it has that constraint of having an end in sight.

JB: I commission myself: like last week, for Maya Angelou's 70th birthday, I loved her so much for so many years, that I simply said, 'I will write her a birthday poem', and I commissioned myself! Because I wanted to speak to her that way. So it includes the two things of commissioning and also writing for, you know, a conversation. And the thing about writing like that is that my greatest pleasure is when you actually do it. And I get it even when I'm writing it, I know it's right, because I have a sense of 'Amen' inside me. And I know when I read it, there's gonna be an 'Amen'. I come from a deeply religious background, and I am still a deeply religious person, despite my rum-drinking ways! (But I find that quite religious too! I'm a religious rum-drinker!) Because when you've been so true to something that, when it comes out of you, you feel an 'Amen', it's the most wonderful feeling in the world, and you don't need an ego trip, and it doesn't bring an ego trip, it brings a great humility, of having humbled yourself so much to someone else's experience, to someone else's voice. Or even if it's your own story, to have even dared to tell it truthfully, you know: you get that resonance where people have felt the same things. And that's one of the reasons why I love women all over the world, because we share so much! And I always say it's not a political choice. I didn't say to God, 'Look, I wanna be born a woman'. This is an amazing gift, I was born a woman, and so I share all these things with women all over the world. And it's kind of wonderful when you get that 'Amen, sister tell it', which is very church. It's a kind of testimony, and you testify for all these voices, and you dare to stand up, like you do in church, and testify, and say, 'Yes, Lord!' And everybody goes, 'Amen, sister, tell it!'

VB: It's really refreshing to hear that kind of statement about there being so much that women share. It just feels like a statement out of time; I haven't heard it for a long time, you know. Recently there's been so much about what women don't share, and about difference . . .

JB: It doesn't matter where I read 'Ordinary Mawning', every woman goes, 'Amen'. And when I say, 'Wish me never did breed, but Lord, you know, me love me children', every woman goes, 'Yes! We wouldn't have admit it, but yes!' And for me, that is it. . . . . everything that I do is about that, you know. Everything that I do is about that.

VB: Do you two feel the same about this connection between women?

JT: Well, when Patience was saying that mostly it's women that come up to her to comment on her work, or buy her books. . . I'm generalizing here, but I think it's true . . . most poetry audiences are predominantly female, because . . . we're the ones that are coming to share.

JB: All poetry readings are predominantly women, yeah.

RH: From my experience at Apples & Snakes, it was always more women than men. No matter what the bill was. I mean, obviously, if it's an all-women bill, you might have the one lone male cowering in the corner. But even on mixed bills, it was predominantly women that would be coming. And I think that is quite true for most poetry readings, actually.

JB: But I read at a Cricket Club dance, and it was men, men, men. And it's one of the lovely things about having a personal culture that is so broad, because I've written a lot about cricket. I have! And there's also wonderful things about how you introduce your poems, because poems that I'd read for women, you know, about loving, and how hard it was, you can just, with a little introduction, make a poem relevant to a completely different audience. So when I went with a poem called, 'Loving Wasn't Easy', into a Cricket Club dance, I dedicated it to all the cricket widows! So all the women in the room, a few of them went 'Amen', and all the men laughed, because they knew it was true! That's one of the differences between the book and the performance, because I can always edit my performances, I change stuff as it's my stuff, I can change it when I feel! And I can make introductions, I can change stories, I can link things differently, which, once you've put a book there, it is so concrete it is frightening. I mean, I love the documentation, and I think my books are very pretty, and I'm glad people buy them, and I think it's nice to cos, you know, I've always read, myself, so I understand books. But what you can do with a stage! And I love how transient it is. I love the fact that whatever happened tonight, could not possibly happen tomorrow night. And why should I think that it should?

RH: I'd agree with you, I think that's what the beauty of it is. If we go back to Murray Laughlan Young, some of the critiques within the mainstream press commented on the fact that they didn't know his work. And I thought, 'Well, why haven't you gone out and seen him perform?' you know, because that's where his work was. There's this assumption, on the part of journalists and literary critics, that the only way you could experience the poet was through the page. The implication was, 'Well, why should we get off our arses and go and see someone do that?' because that isn't a valid place to experience poetry, and I think that says quite a lot about this particular English culture's attitude towards poetry. There's lots of things I like about poetry in performance: the fact that it's communal, it's bringing people together, it stops the isolation, and it's saying that poets are actually out there within communities, with audiences, making contact with people, because the dominant perception of poetry is of the poet as isolated, and the reader is isolated. . . You can be just as intimate within an audience; it is direct communication to you, as an individual within a social environment. I mean, that's what I enjoy about all this.

JB: And I find that there is no less a love of language in my performance. I love it when you see people close their eyes, and begin to experience everything through the ear, and the sense of what the voice can do. It was interesting, I went and did a festival last year, in this wonderful full theatre. I love theatres because you can do everything in a theatre, and they've thought about the acoustics. And the person who invited me, the organizer, said, 'Come and talk to the stage manager and the sound man, so that they can fix your microphone. And you'll need a long cord', he said, 'won't you?' And I said, 'No, no, no, no, the lectern is fine with the microphone there, because I don't move'. He said, 'You don't move?' And it was obvious that he had booked me into this very English festival as the kind of poet who was gonna come in and move about, because I was a performance poet, and he was so disappointed when I turned down a long microphone lead for the lectern and the mike on the lectern. I said, 'I don't move. But just wait, it still will be a performance.' And, you know, the idea that one has to be cavorting around the stage to be a performance poet! Cos I find stillness has been my greatest help over the years, so that when one makes one move. . . Maya Angelou, you've got to watch her, she has mastered that, you know. One finger nail is enough, when you're still! Whereas if you start jumping across the stage, the language has gone, it's really difficult. And so I'm very very still on the stage. And I find that the slower and stiller I get, the more of a chance the audience gets to actually find the language. So I'm against a concept of performance as something that is largely visual, and something that has to do a lot, and excite you all the time that way. I think it's about the voice. The poetry performance is about the voice. And first of all, seducing the air, through all the techniques of voice, so that people want to listen. And once you've got them seduced, then the language becomes the main focus, which is why I prefer performing solo to performing with a reggae band, because you lose the language. Unless you're so well known that people are reciting your poems, because they've got the album at home! In which case, great! But you lose that sense of language, because so much is happening musically, and with all the band on stage with you, and all of that. And you've got to go for sound more than meaning. But in a solo performance, what you can do with language . . . with the voice heightening stuff, the voice can give you all the double meanings, just what you do with your voice. Ideal.

RH: Are you invited to a certain type of venue, do you think? And do you think there are other reasons than because of your writing that you're actually being invited there? Especially, for instance, Black History Month: I mean, is it just because you're black that you're being invited, or is it because of your work, and how has that pigeon-holed you and your work? Or would you rather get rid of all those things that are carried with that term, 'performance poet', and just be invited as a poet in your own right, as any other writer on that literary circuit – especially literature festivals – is being invited?

JB: Well, quite frankly, honey, invite me anywhere! You know, if there is a wall, then I'll melt that too! You know me, I go everywhere that I'm invited.

RH: Well, that's what I'm getting at. My perception as a programmer, as the one who's been the intermediary, is that people book not because of the work, but because of other reasons. You're a woman poet, or you're a black woman poet, or you're a lesbian poet, or you're this, or you're that, and they're booking under Equal Opps., basically.

PA: I know what you mean. A lot of the time I don't know why they book me. Usually there's somebody there who's seen me perform before. That happens a lot. I know I get asked to do things because people just like what I do, and, yeah, I'm sure also it's great for them because it fits into their remit, you know. Perhaps it's cocky of me, but I like to think I get asked to do it, because I tend to do a good job, generally. But yeah, I'm sure there's all those machinations behind the scenes.

JB: You see, for me, the relevant thing is not about why I've been asked, or whether people might have the right conceptions or the wrong ones. What concerns me is the group of people who have actually turned up to the reading. So the organizers might be crap, and might be completely politically off-centre, but I'm not too into that. For me, it's a miracle that anybody picks themselves up out of their house, and says they are going to a poetry reading! And my entire allegiance is to those people. There are some times you meet organizers who have, like, killed themselves to try and get me an audience, and you love them so dearly that you work, because you realize that this person has a genuine love of poetry, and is working damned hard in that community to put something together, so you give them everything you've got, out of support, you know, and you go for four-hour dinners afterwards and kind of pep them up! Buy a rum! But their allegiance is to whoever has come, you know. I mean, I went and did one gig once, and they'd heard that I did work with Survivors' Poetry, and that I'd written poems about madness. And all these mentally and physically handicapped people came in their wheelchairs, and they were sitting there, and I had no idea whether they understood

41

or anything, because, you know, they've got faces that you can't tell, sometimes . . .

JT: And you can't read their eyes . . .

JB: . . . what's going on, and you can't read anything. And I thought, 'Mmm!' And I went completely for sound. I chose all the poems that I thought would soothe, by the way they sounded, not necessarily meaning. So I didn't start reading poems about being mentally ill, I just chose sound things that I thought would be really soothing, because it was the only thing I could do.

JT: And you didn't know until you got there?

JB: I didn't know till I got there. It was the only thing I could do out of . . . this is who has come. 'What can I do for you?' And, like, I said, I'm an old church girl, and 'where two or three are gathered together in Thy name there will I be also'. I'm an old church girl, I can't help it! I just felt, well, you know, 'Some soothing sound might be welcome here'. And I sung a lot. I put some songs in.

JT: There was one of your questions that was about identity: do we feel pigeon-holed, or that we're booked because of where we're from. And I have felt, often, in the past, that I'm tokenized. At the same time, I'm getting paid, and at the same time, I'm doing the work, and so, you know, I get around that. But I have felt it oftentimes. And then there's the thing of me being Maori, and people not really knowing what that is, and I need to do a 'haka' (war dance), and make a lot of noise and have to be fierce. You can get beyond that and begin to change misconceptions through the performance. But yeah, I do feel that way sometimes.

PA: I do think there's often an assumption, with performance poetry, that the person's got to be black, or of colour, or certainly not white English. There's this perception that we do it better, because we're more 'natural performers'.

JB: Have you seen John Cooper Clarke?

PA: Yeah, exactly. But there is a general misconception . . . I do believe that a lot of people believe that.

RH: I think they do.

PA: Our colour goes in our favour, in terms of getting more gigs.

RH: Yeah. Apples & Snakes which puts forward a multi-cultural plat-form, is basically known for black poets. But that wasn't the case, what they actually did. Now the only reason I can think why that happened is because, perhaps, it was one of the first platforms to actually programme that way. And that's the image that's been picked up. And so then people disregarded anything else that the organization did, and what it was trying to put forward: the idea of performance poetry as being a very broad church, going from the very abstract poets like Bob Cobbing, all the way through to John Hegley, going right across the spectrum. So I think what's happened with performance poetry is that, as you say, it's associated with black poets, and it's also associated with comic cabaret poetry, and then all the other kind of inflections right across the board seem to be disappearing. I came across a document from a Regional Arts Board recently, in which, for the Performance Poetry Award, the definition of performance poetry is comedy and cabaret. Now, where the hell they've got that from, I've no idea. I just cringed when I read it. And I thought, 'Well, this has obviously been written by a bureaucrat somewhere in an Arts Board, who has never actually seen it, and has just heard certain people talk about it', and you just think, well, 'No, that isn't what it's about'.

JB: I would say I am as far away from that as you could get!

RH: What disturbed me about seeing that document was that they were working towards a definition, which would then be passed around the Arts funding system, and which would then say . . . 'Well, this is performance poetry'; it's being institutionalized as this. They're saying, if you're looking for performance poetry, these are the elements that you should be looking for.

PA: Well, I could be being really cynical, but perhaps they did that deliberately, hoping that more white poets would take part.

RH: But who's to say that white poets should be cabaret and comedy anyway?

PA: I know, but the public perception of successful white poet equals John Hegley, John Cooper Clarke and Joolz. All use stand-up techniques in their acts. Therefore, more white poets tend to take that route.

JT: Jem Rolls (from the 'Big Word' Club venue, London) said to me the other day, 'there's so few women poets who do comedy'. And I said, 'Our department is the heart level. We leave the comedy to the guys, really, to keep their front up!'

RH: But I think also what's happening within the performance poetry scene is that it has actually narrowed its field as well. It is defining itself by certain things. I don't think it's as broad as it used to be, in what it promotes. I mean, in style terms, and the performers who are being used.

JB: I'm not even sure I like the term 'performance poetry'. Does it mean I don't have to go on the stage to read poems, because I can just get up there and dance? I mean, I understand 'poets in performance', but 'performance poets', really, I am not so sure about the term at all. I don't know how it became the term, but I really do expect that the poems will just get up and do it themselves, every time I hear it!

PA: The comedy scene has developed; it's huge, people get paid – even if you're at a lowish level – you can get paid better money than some of the poetry scenes. Some male poets I spoke to said, 'Well, we're more likely to do gigs for the comedy scene', even though they like doing the poetry. I mean, they might do some poetry on the comedy scene interspersed with the stand-up stuff, but their reality is that comedy pays the rent, while poetry pays for pints.

JT: Wasn't Richard Allan a comedian before he became a poet? Who realized that what he was writing could be defined as performance poetry?

RH: Well, I think it's quite interesting going back ten years or so: people who are now household names – Mark Hurst, Phil Jupitus – they were poets. I mean, they were comic poets, but they were poets. And Mark Steele, who writes in the *Guardian* now. Well, they've now all made it. John Hegley is really the only one who actually still goes out there and does it as poetry, and does it as live performance. He's the only one who hasn't shifted that a great deal, and he earns a very good living.

JB: At the same time, I love John Hegley's stuff. He's okay on the page, you can get it, but John Hegley in performance: he's the kind of poet I go to see! But I've seen poets, because of audience pressure, change from really sensitive material, and I think a lot of John Hegley's material is very sensitive, it's just his way of expressing it. But I've seen poets who feel they have to entertain, they've accepted that pressure on them to be this thing called, 'performance poet', and lost that wonderful, lovely sense of detail, lovely sense of tender things that were happening in their work, and have gone completely for the one-liners.

RH: I think there are various things going on there, and this is about pragmatism, isn't it? My perception of the poetry scene is that there's very little infrastructure there. There's only certain ways you can move about in it. And therefore, if you actually do want to earn a living within an artistic medium, however you wanna define that, then you might have to broaden yourself out, especially within the comedy scene, so it's far more lucrative to become a comic.

JB: You get booked again if you make the punters laugh!

RH: Yes. Because there is a far bigger infrastructure and a support structure there, than there is for poets. You know, to actually make a career as a poet, I'd say, is pretty difficult. There's an issue here about patronage, it brings in compromises. I mean, to get on certain platforms in this country, in poetry, do you feel that you would have to compromise your own work? I mean the more 'hard-line' literature festivals, like Hay-on-Wye, for example. . .

VB: But that conservative understanding of what poetry is . . . that's what dominates all academic circles, I think.

JB: Yeah, but poetry . . . any art, is going to remain subjective. And when people begin to have power over festivals and all that, they bring their own personal likes and dislikes. And I think one of the wonderful things about the arts is that there is room for everyone. And if people like that kind of stuff, and that's the festival they wanna go to, then, you know, all power to them. I've never seen my role as having to . . . I've just continued doing what I'm doing, and who books me, books me. I've never seen that I had to break in to a house someone has set up. If that's the way they wanna live in their house, then thank you, I am quite comfortable in mine. You know, I mean, if you invite me over, I'm going to be a very charming guest, but I don't want to beat your door down, I'm not in the least bit interested in beating your door down. I have a very very comfortable home of my own, you know.

PA: When my next book comes out, I definitely want to be on the literature festivals, and if I'm not on the literature festivals, I want to know why. So I probably will be banging on some doors! Who knows!

JT: But you probably will be at those festivals.

PA: I don't know. How do I know? You worked on some of the publicity for the book, you know that wasn't easy, was it, just trying to get reviews?

RH: No, it wasn't.

PA: That was the first book, but I know that when book number two comes out I'll want to be booked for the key literature festivals. And I know that, as a performance poet, some people would just hear the term 'performance poet', and they wouldn't wanna know.

VB: Do you send your work to the National Poetry Competition? Have you tried to get an Eric Gregory Award? Have you tried for any of the albeit limited but existing grants that are available for poets?

JT: No.

VB: Why not?

PA: Well, I've tried one or two, but I didn't get anywhere.

JT: I'm waiting until I have something ready for publication; then I might attempt to do that. But also, I think it's a lot easier if you've already published something.

PA: What about competitions, though?

JT: I'm not gonna pay someone, I'm not gonna pay to have my work read, No. What I like, is when the Native Women in the Arts, in Canada, hears about me, and writes me and asks me to submit something . . . they don't ask me to pay for it. They invite me to be a part of something that means something to me – indigenous women, internationally.

VB: So is it actually, then, that you don't see the relevance of trying to get an entrée into a context that has no resonance for you?

JT: No. No.

RH: You'd rather aim yourself where you feel . . .

JT: If they call me, I'll consider it, and I will tailor a performance I do to what I feel is appropriate: my more structured, or formal work, or whatever.

JB: No, you mustn't do that!

JT: Well, that's what I'm saying: we all have a range in our work, and it's like, as you said, you don't walk into a classroom full of 10-year-old boys and start performing erotic poetry is what I'm saying. So I bring –

JB: But they'd love it!

JT: Yeah, but I'd have mayhem on my hands.

JB: I think, as a writer, I carry some responsibility. . . especially coming from an island like Jamaica, and coming out of the black British experience, where not enough has been written yet, it's not something that I chose politically, I just happen to write that way. And I write for lots of women like me, lots of women who have gone through things like me, and I bring all these people with me, and so anywhere they're going to let me in, they're letting in all these women that I bring.

RH: I heard Patience on Radio 4 with Jenny Murray, and she mentioned the phrase 'political poetry', because that's another thing that's thrown at performance poets, and black poets: basically, you don't fit into the canon, because you write political stuff, you have a social agenda, or you're political, and that's used as a dismissal of the work. The Western canon is founded on a pure aesthetic; we don't actually approach any of these agendas within our work . . . well, there's two questions coming out of that. Do you encounter levels of dismissal of the work that you do, and also, do you see yourself as having an overt or covert political and social agenda, when you're actually doing your work?

JT: Yes!

PA: I can comment on the last issue as well, about competitions. One of the reasons I haven't entered competitions is, I've read the ones that win. There's something in the *Independent on Sunday*, and I just thought, 'Well, I don't write stuff like that. My stuff's much more hard-hitting . . . and so they're not even likely to consider it.' So that's why I've tended to shy away from them. I have often been accused, 'Your stuff is political'. I remember someone coming up to me, and saying, 'That's just anger'; of *Sentences* they said, 'That's anger, that's not poetry'. And I said, 'Well, do you wanna sit down with me, and I'll tell you how I wrote it, I'll give you some of the references, and explain the rhythm and rhyme structure', and they didn't like that at all. So I do think that's used a lot to dismiss performance poetry. I'm not for art for art's sake, personally, although I believe it must exist, but every single thing I write, there's a very strong reason for writing it, and there's an even stronger reason for thinking that anybody out there might want to listen to it. So I've sat down and written sonnets I wouldn't show anybody. I like form, actually, but I think if you want to put it out there, you want something that you find really fascinating or interesting as a subject, then that's the reason for putting it out, and it's gotta be well written. It's like, for me, the two are inextricably linked. But I always say, 'Well, if politics was the primary thing, then I'd join the local council, because I think I could do better there'. But seriously, I am a poet, first and foremost.

JB: Poetry, whatever the subject matter, is ultimately about an interesting use of language, and it can be any subject matter, it's just really about what you're doing with language. And I do think that there is something in the criticism about black poetry. I'm sure it happens in other poetry as well, where it is accepted that it is enough to make a right-on black statement, or a right-on political statement, to rhyme, and you repeat it as often as possible.

PA: That was in the eighties!

JB: I think it does happen. And then . . . women did that right-on kind of feminist thing, and you begin to wonder, where is the love of language in this? And you could be saying exactly the same things, but with such a love of language that you would know at once that it's poetry.

PA: Yes, yes, I completely agree.

JB: So I don't think it's down to subject matter. And I think there is room for the criticism.

PA: Yeah, I do think that, in the seventies and eighties, a lot of the stuff that was coming through was very closely linked with political movements.

JB: I've met people like that, who are really really brilliant at packaging their product and getting it out there. And, as a result, you get quite good poets being dismissed, as a result of how prolific, and well produced these what I call 'propaganda poets' are. And for me, propaganda is a great thing, because, you know, I'm very into political activism. But I wouldn't say political propaganda is poetry. . . but it should not be used to dismiss all the fine work that is, in fact, happening, that may be political in nature.

RH: Obviously, I'm coming from a completely different perspective to you: I'm an administrator, having worked in poetry. I've seen it as one of my purposes, having worked within that, to actually break down those barriers, to break down those levels of dismissal and the perceptions of what poetry is, because I'm having to speak to these people, and deal with that right at the edge, really. So those are quite dominant issues for me. How do I help the poets that I'm actually working with? How can I help them develop their career, so that they have more money, and they can get their work where they want their work to be? And therefore, you know, I've had to confront those things.

JB: Well, you see, what I established from very early on, was a series of bottom lines. The first bottom line I established, way back in the seventies, which I'd learnt a bit from childhood, was: I know how to plant my own food. That was my first bottom line. If all else failed, I could feed myself. I know how to grow things to eat, and I'm pretty good, if it comes to that, at keeping chickens, if I need some extra protein! That was my first bottom line on this route to becoming a writer. My second bottom line was that I trained as a teacher, so that if all else failed, I quite like teaching, and I'd still be working with language: I could go and teach. And on the strength of those two, I then decided, 'Okay, I'll write!' But I'm not writing on the basis of making any serious compromises about what I do at all. What I do is what I do, and my allegiance is to the voices that speak through me. I just could not possibly be dishonest about that, or laugh at my own people that I bring, or in any way undermine the movement of which I am a product and a part. So my bottom lines are there. And for writing, well, writing couldn't ask me to do that, because I'm doing it personally, but if performance ever expected that of me, then, you know, I'll go all the way back to my bottom lines. You know, if making money out of it had to do that to me: then no, not at all. Not at all. Cos nobody can stop your poetry, and I'm quite happy just getting drunk with my mates and coming up with something, you know. It may not be as rewarding financially, but in terms of keeping one's spirit alive it is very very rewarding! Well, thank God I haven't had to make the choice. I've never had to compromise about what I write, or where I perform it. Maybe if I had to do a poem about oral sex in front of a fundamental Rastafarian audience, I might disappear through the door! But . . .

JT: I think it's true to say that most of the people I know on the poetry scene are not about to be compromised in what they're doing. Most of the people I observe to be very focused, very driven, and I don't think they're easily swayed.

PA: They would be if they were offered a British Airways advert! That's the latest one that's going round now. Virgin's been done, so what would you do if BA dangled fifty grand in front of you? Very few poets I spoke to gave an absolute no!

VB: Is there any overlap between the circuit you were talking about – the performance circuit, which, I guess, is predominantly London-based, but travelling – and the more traditional poetry on the page, national poetry competitions, Eric Gregory Awards, Carcanet Press, you know, that more . . .

JT: I guess because I'm not from here, not 'English', part of me is intimidated by this whole Poetry Society other-world, and then part of me just feels, 'I'll get to that if and when the opportunity arises, if the time is right', and we're resonating on the same level and everything else. But I'm more recently beginning to feel resentful that there is that divide, that I might have to work very hard to make a foray into that world, if I choose to. But I wanted to say that I feel that 'LitPop' which happened recently, went quite some way into breaking down that divide. The audience was amazing on the nights when I was there. It was three nights of that, so powerful and intense. I don't know if that's been done many times before, that deliberate crossing, throwing these two elements together . . .

RH: I think it has been done, whether it's been done successfully is another matter. From my experience of programming for Apples & Snakes, if you stuck to a concept, like all-women, or an all-Caribbean event, or an all-abstract poetry, or whatever, then you would have a given audience, basically. But then if you crossed over, either stylistically or actually programmed black poets with white poets, then the audience just . . . you lost it somewhere. Something happens. The audiences at Apples & Snakes, for each week, could be completely different. It had a very high level of first-time attenders: 50 per cent of the audience would be first-time attenders to the gig. Now, that doesn't happen in theatre, it doesn't happen in other art forms. I suppose from my perspective as administrator, that's amazing, because it's one of the very few art forms which is actually getting to new audiences, and has got a very young audience profile as well. These are all the big sticking points when you look at 'the arts': the fact that they

FEMINIST REVIEW NO 62, SUMMER 1999

don't have a young audience profile, and they can't get new audiences. For me, then, poetry is a very dynamic art form which can reach a lot of different people, right across the board when you examine the demographics, be it age, education, whatever. And that's why I'm far more interested in stage poetry than page poetry, because the usual audience for page poetry is 50+, university-educated, and it's all the standard things you'd expect really. Certain organizations have broken down all of that, but the thing that really gets me is, that's never been acknowledged at any level; that type of work is not acknowledged in any way, really. And, if anything, is seen as a threat, because we're treading on their ground, and . . . I don't see it that way.

VB: And it's the performances that get the big audiences.

RH: Yeah.

PA: I was asked, last year, to do quite a few workshops for more for traditional page poets, to give them performance skills.

RH: In the Green Paper on poetry, which has just been done, which is going to set forward the Arts Council poetry policy, it has this whole section about how poets should be trained in performance techniques. Then it goes on to say 'the growth areas of poetry are women's poetry, and performance poetry'. Performance poetry is defined as black, and then it says, 'but, of course, at this time, we don't have any money for these areas'. These are the growth areas, but actually we're going to concentrate on the press that only sells two copies! I'm being facetious, but, at the end of the day, that's what it means, you know; it means that the poets who have come through the competitions, who have gone into Carcanet or whatever press (and there aren't that many that are just purely poetry-based), they're going to help them.

JB: And what's incredible is that performance poetry has actually rescued the whole concept of poetry from there. Poets who work in schools amaze me, because what they've done is taken poetry from kids' 'Hate Department', with mushy peas on the menu in the lunch canteen and all the things that people hate about school: poetry was in that list! But performance poetry has changed all that, and several generations of people will now buy a book of poems, because of performance poets, who have not been published!

PA: I think school work is amazing. . . not just the work I've done as an individual poet, but knowing certain poets who have been doing it for fifteen, twenty years, going to schools, it's just fascinating. To see the transformation that takes place!

RH: But also it's a broadening out of conceptions of what poetry is. I know a lot of the work Paul does in schools with poetry; he has a whole poetry course, and he starts off with Benjamin Zephaniah.

JB: And they love it! Anyone who can conceive of poetry, without some sense, however minute, of music, is not talking poetry at all, you know. Maybe an advanced crossword puzzle, but it's certainly not poetry!

VB: Are there areas that you'd like to talk about that we haven't strayed into?

JB: Yes, why I write in my kitchen!

VB: Would you like to go into that a little bit?

JB: I write in my kitchen, because it is where everyone gathers. And if I were to wait for complete silence, a private study somewhere, I probably would not write a word! I mean, I love silence and all of that, but, over the years, I've shaped myself to welcoming whoever walks into my space while I'm enjoying my silence.

JT: I think that's really incredible.

JB: Because I'm the mother of three children, and I have a big family, and, yes, you can find so much silence, and it's wonderful when everyone goes, and you have some silence. But, you know, I've still been able to work with people coming in and out of my life. And I love it. And what it also gives you, and I think that's because we voice things. Because you can always say, 'Hey, listen to this, I've just written this'. And I edit through sound, I don't edit on the page. I edit through sound. I read stuff aloud, and I know when the music is at fault in the sound, and if the music is at fault in the sound, the word you've chosen is wrong. Always, music is a wonderful way of editing poetry.

VB: Are there poets who have been particularly influential for you?

PA: Oh God, where do I start! I suppose, in the early days, I saw Benjamin Zephaniah, and I thought, as a performer, he was fantastic. And as a person, he was very supportive of me and my development as a poet. And he kept telling me to get a book out, and Merle Collins as well, especially in the really early days. She was in African Dawn then, I found that quite interesting, her working with African music. And also Lemn Sissay: in terms of my contemporaries, Lemn's probably been the most exciting, supportive poet. We've done loads of gigs together; people seem to like the package, the two of us, so that's been really brilliant. I can name zillions more, you know, – Jean Breeze, and Ahmed Sheikh who was in African Dawn years ago, you know, a lot of that generation really inspired me.

JB: Well, you know, in terms of stage, the woman who towered above all other women on the stage was Maya Angelou. That woman knows what a stage is about.

JT: And can use it.

RH: I saw her years ago at Lewisham Theatre, which is a vacuum, it really is a place! And I was right at the back in the balcony, and she walks on, and she's very tall and statuesque, and, in fact, she just filled it, you know. And just one person filling a space like that . . . I could barely see her, really, but you just felt that she was talking to you, as an individual, with, you know, 2,000 people. Well, that is an amazing gift to have! So that you can be in that space, and yet feel that you're being talked to personally. And it goes back to what Jean was saying. She just shimmered on, you know. It was absolutely amazing. Amazing what she did.

JB: You've got to be coming from somewhere, because performance is not a shell, it's not something you take up and put on and go on stage. A stage is just somewhere you walk through on your journey through life, and you bring everything of where you are coming from, and you leave whatever you leave, but you go with it, it's a part of the walk. And I think one of the reasons why there are embarrassing performances, is that people think that the stage is this place, and it then begins to impact on all kind of power levels, and your politics get seriously disturbed if you look at it like that. And for me, my most comfortable place (outside of my kitchen) is the stage, because it is just somewhere I walk through on that journey, and when I get there, I begin with being there. So it's not about performing for, that's why the word is disturbing, because it's not . . . If you're gonna 'perform' without bringing all of that journey with you, it does not work, and it can be awfully embarrassing.

PA: I just wanted to say something about slams, in terms of what Jean was saying about the audience being really important. I co-judged a National Slam with John Cooper Clarke, and others. It was really exciting, giving marks for performance. We were allowed to give a little bit of our judgement, but a lot of it had to reflect the audience response. We didn't have a clapometer, some of the US slams have a clapometer so they can accurately measure the applause! What I found especially interesting was that the four pieces I thought were absolutely excellent, the audience gave a standing ovation. I was really in tune with the audience. And I do think, in terms of growth and poetry, that performance poets need feedback in terms of not just normal applause, but that slam applause, where the audience actually knows that they are literally part of the judging process. Also, slams attract huge audiences and up-and-coming poets need to reach people to build their profile.

JB: I think it's always interesting the way each generation decides how it's going to deal with poetry. I'm 42 years, so I'm kind of middling, and I know how difficult it was sometimes with a generation ahead of you thinking, 'Oooh', you are kind of ruining the purist of poetry, and, luckily, I had others, as I said, who didn't do that. But we all have our personal likes and dislikes. There's a lot of stuff I, personally, don't like, but if the generation that is creating it, that is what they like, then they have every right, just as my generation had every right to do what it did. And for that reason, I love slams, because that's what this present generation has created with poetry, and I think it's brilliant, because the kind of audiences that you see at slams, you never see anywhere else.

PA: Those people never go to bog standard poetry gigs.

JB: And that's great. That's great. It's the fast food of poetry. But like my mother always said, you know, when this fast food argument came up, because she likes Kentucky Fried Chicken, and she always said, 'Well, if I fry some chicken here, and fry up some potatoes, and some coleslaw, it's supposed to be good for you, but if you go . . . ! Why is Kentucky, then, not any good for you? Because it's a piece of chicken, some potatoes and some coleslaw.' So I have that kind of feeling: yes, this is fast food, it's like that, you know.

JT: That was really how I got started was in slams, just because that's what was happening, and that was a way to get started. And I remember, even then, feeling different, because I'd get up there for my two poems, and instead of launching into it, and bashing it out, I did my poems in my way, which is not strident. It's more fluid. And I realized that, wait a minute, this is only something that people have taken on, some kind of an idea that they have. You have your time, you do your poetry. You choose. You choose to do with that time whatever you will, and I started to like slams more, because I realized that you didn't have to conform; the space was there. And then slam started to relax, so that it was more just about an arena for poetry. And there was the excitement there; there was a level of competition that adds an edge. It was a very early lesson in learning how to go against the grain, to stand out. You could almost make more of an impression by standing still for a second of your precious seconds.

JB: And I think it's a lot more honest a competition than poetry prizes, where you have a set of judges, who are supposed to know everything there is about poetry. I've done it. I know how difficult it is. Saying, 'Well, this is the one in this year . . . for Britain'

JT: Also, in a slam, you could win one night, and do the same thing the

FEMINIST REVIEW NO 62, SUMMER 1999

next night and crash. . . so there was no real ego attached to it. And a great sense of camaraderie as well, in amongst this.

PA: Yeah, definitely. Definitely.

Notes

This discussion was organized by Ruth Harrison, and recorded at her home in South London in May 1998. Ruth is a poetry programmer who has extensive experience of the performance scene in London. She has worked for the pioneering poetry promoters, Apples & Snakes, and as a freelance programmer and promoter, and is currently working on a research project about women poets whose main medium is performance.

Jean Binta Breeze is a Jamaican poet, resident in Britain since 1985. She has performed at festivals all over the world. A trained actor and experienced performer and poet, Breeze is also a very popular workshop leader. She has published *Spring Cleaning* (Virago) and recordings of her work include *Tracks*. She has also written the screenplay for several films, including *Hallelujah Anyhow*!

Patience Agbabi is based in London, although she has performed in many countries. Influenced by rap, ska and blues as well as page-based poetic tradition, she is well known for her writing workshops as well as her involvement in several innovative poetry video projects. Her first collection, *R.A.W.* was published by Gecko Press in 1995. Her work is sharply attuned to political realities of the 1990s, defying easy definitions of 'Black' and 'female'. She is a member of the performance group, Atomic Lip, and is currently working on her second book, while continuing to perform at a wide range of festivals and venues.

Jillian Tipene is a Maori poet who left Aotearoa (New Zealand) fifteen years ago, and has been living and working in New York and London since. She writes and performs poetry that is deeply influenced by her Nga Puhi, Te Rarawa and Irish descent. Her work is a fusion of spiritual, musical and poetic impulses. She is also a director, most notably of mixed-media theatre, and her own one-woman show, inspired by Frida Kahlo, played for four weeks at the Edinburgh Festival in 1997.

Two Poems

Patience Agbabi

FEMINIST REVIEW NO 62, SUMMER 1999, ISSN 0141-7789, PP. 55–57

These poems come from a series of sestinas. The sestina has a complex pattern of repeated line-ends: only six words are used, and the end-word of one stanza forms/recurs as the end-word of the first line of the next.

Ms De Meanour

It's midnight. Party time,
time for a girl
to hit the West End
so hard it weeps like a child,
lover boy.
Don't you just adore the dark,

the funky smell of the dark?
Midnight chimes. Time
for boy
meets girl
in the mirror and wild child
bitch with a dick from Crouch End

becomes Wild West End
diva with dark
luscious lashes, courtesy of every child's
dream fairy godmother. Time
to lose the glass slipper, Cinderella. Diamonds are a girl's
best friend and boy

oh boy,
I'm harder than a brickie from Mile End!
A girl's gotta do what a girl's
gotta do. Strap it in before the pumpkin carriage beeps its dark

FEMINIST REVIEW NO 62, SUMMER 1999

bulbous time-
to-hit-the-road horn. Now I'm a child,

the bastard child
of Barbara Cartland and Boy
George, in a sequined shift, checking the time
on a rolex. I hear the wheels hit the end
of the street and I dive into the dark.
Go girl!

Strut your funky stuff, girl!
Cos the night's a hyperactive child
on E129 and the dark
is every boy's
sheath. West End
is where it's at and the time

is ripe for boys
who are girls
in the dark.

Martina

I must have been sweet sixteen at the time,
boyish, straight up straight down. She was the girl
next door but one, living at the dark end
of the street, the fat ugly duckling child
who grew up gorgeous. A different boy
for each day of the week. She was a dark

horse, kept herself to herself, her sloe-dark
eyes revealing nothing. It was war time
and rations chiselled our features but boy,
she kept her curves. I was a grown-up girl,
she was woman. Time had silenced the child
in her eyes. We prayed for the war to end

in our Sunday best. But we were weekend
disciples, evacuees scared of dark
nights pierced with blitzkrieg pyrotechnics, child-
like, clinging to mother's skirt. She found time
to party in seamed stockings, good time girl
growing voluptuous from man and boy,

full-bosomed and broad-hipped. I was tomboy
running errands, climbing trees till the end.
But she was the midnight rouge glamour girl
who french-kissed GI lovers in the dark
whispering, 'come up and see me some time'.
She was wicked woman: I was wild child.

We all knew she was expecting a child.
In those days we all expected the boy
to marry her. But, it being war time,
her dangerous liaison had to end.
Her father threw her out into pitch-dark
November's embrace with the words 'no girl

of mine . . .' She gave birth to a baby girl,
Martina. They wanted to put the child
up for adoption. Tina had the dark
features of her father, the soldier boy
pierced deep with love's fierce arrow till the end,
bleeding dry on a battlefield. In time,

she got married for the child's sake, a boy-
next-door type; and in time I met a girl
with sloe-dark eyes and loved her till the end.

Dilemmas and Developments:
Eavan Boland Re-examined

Sarah Maguire

FEMINIST REVIEW NO 62, SUMMER 1999, ISSN 0141-7789, PP. 58–66

Abstract

In 'The Woman Poet: Her Dilemma' (1986–7), the Irish poet Eavan Boland argued that women poets were obstructed on the one hand by traditional ideas of femininity and poetry, and on the other by the demands of separatist feminism. In 'Dilemmas and Developments: Eavan Boland Re-examined' Sarah Maguire argues that in recent years women poets have clearly achieved greater confidence as a result of changes in their audience. However, the underlying dilemma facing a woman poet – that of the tension between the demands of femininity and the role expected of a post-Romantic lyric poet – continues to remain unresolved.

Keywords

women poets; lyric poetry; post-romanticism; subjectivity; feminism; literary establishment

In 1986, the Winter edition of *Stand* magazine carried a small – six-page – article by the Irish poet, Eavan Boland. It was called, 'The Woman Poet: Her Dilemma', and it was Boland's attempt to address the issues which feminism had recently stirred up about the position of women poets. This was a hotly-debated subject at the time. Only the year before, I'd had a furious argument with Craig Raine, then the new poetry editor at Faber, as to why Faber published no living women poets. 'Because there aren't any good enough', he'd flatly informed me. Two years on, in 1987, Raine himself oversaw the publication of *The Faber Book of 20th Century Women's Poetry*, edited by Fleur Adcock (dogged by rumours that his editing style had verged on the intrusive), which followed Carol Rumens' selection, *Making for the Open: The Chatto Book of Post-Feminist Poetry 1964–1984*. As Boland's article – and the appearance of these two anthologies from 'establishment' publishing houses – makes plain, feminism had started to trouble the literary mainstream in Ireland and Britain.[1]

The authors of these three key texts of the mid-1980s which attempt to breach the gap between feminism and the poetry establishment all share a set of assumptions, an agenda – and an identity. They are all women. They are all respected poets writing within the literary mainstream. They have all been affected by feminism. They want to draw attention to the specific difficulties faced by women poets, to plead a special case, but they also want poetry written by women to be judged simply as poetry. 'The danger is', writes Adcock, 'that women's poetry will be shunted into a ghetto, occupying the "Women's" section of the bookshop rather than the poetry section, and taught in "Women's Studies" courses at universities rather than literature courses' (Adcock, 1987: 2). And Carol Rumens, rather touchingly, hopes that,

> the fact that the women represented here are, first and foremost, good poets will be noted equally by those who think there are no women poets of any merit, and by those generous souls who believe that women should be judged by less than stringent measurements of excellence.
>
> (Rumens, 1985: xviii)

These anxious and defensive comments are clearly part of the 'dilemma' Eavan Boland sought to address. So what is this dilemma, as Boland perceives it? And has the position of women poets in Ireland and Britain changed over the past decade?

At the beginning of her article,[2] Boland herself tells us,

> The dilemma I speak of is inherent in a shadowy but real convergence between new experience and an established aesthetic. What this means in practical terms is that the woman poet today is caught in a field of force. Powerful, persuasive voices are in her ear as she writes. Distorting and simplifying ideas of womanhood and poetry fall as shadows between her and the courage of her own experience. If she listens to these voices, yields to these ideas, her work will be obstructed. If, however, she evades the issue, runs for cover and pretends there is no pressure, then she is likely to lose the resolution she needs to encompass the critical distance between writing poems and being a poet. A distance which for women is fraught in any case, as I hope to show, with psychosexual fear and doubt.
>
> (Boland, 1997: 239–40)

What is interesting about Boland's approach is precisely her attention to the 'psychosexual' as a field for explanation of the dilemma she wishes to analyse. Adcock and Rumens don't do this. They don't do this partly I imagine because they're both writing short introductions to their respective anthologies which have enough other issues to cover in a small space. When they do touch on the anomalous position of women poets, they both seem to come down in favour of discrimination in social practices as a suitable explanation. 'What is different about poetry by women, of course, is not its nature but the fact that until recently it has been undervalued and to some extent neglected', as Adcock puts it (Adcock, 1987: 1).

But Boland is more ambitious. In order to analyse the psychosexual field of force in which women poets find themselves, she presents a theory she calls the 'Romantic Heresy'. This, she explains, 'is not romanticism proper, although it is related to it', and she quotes Lionel Trilling's famous dictum that, 'Before Wordsworth poetry had a subject. After Wordsworth its prevalent subject was the poet's own subjectivity' (Boland, 1997: 241). This, for Boland, means that, 'poets are distinctive not so much because they write poetry as because in order to do so, they have poetic feelings about poetic experiences' (Boland, 1997: 241). But the problem for her is not so much about the arena of 'poetic feelings', but that 'poetic experiences' have been narrowly defined to exclude the ordinary, everyday experiences shared by most women. Housework, by definition, is not a 'poetic experience'. What worries Boland is that, because of this effective 'exclusion zone' defining the post-romantic canon, women poets may be tempted to 'romanticize these routines and these feelings so as to align them with what is considered poetic' (Boland, 1997: 242), by which I imagine she means that women poets will be tempted to invest their banal routines with portentous emotional fervour, leading to a failure of authenticity. (Interestingly, this very criticism has been levelled at some of Boland's own 'domestic' poems.)

But there is more. Assailing the woman poet from another side is the ideology of what we've now learned to call, 'political correctness', although this was an unknown term in the dark ages of the mid-1980s. Instead, Boland calls this impulse 'separatist' and she argues that these

> separatist prescriptions demand that women be true to the historical angers which underwrite the women's movement, that they cast aside preexisting literary traditions, that they evolve not only their own writing but the criteria by which to judge it.
>
> (Boland, 1997: 243)

And she concludes that, 'the gradual emphasis on the appropriate subject matter and the correct feelings has become as constricting and corrupt within feminism as within romanticism' (Boland, 1997: 243).

Boland's quarrel here is with Adrienne Rich, whom she quotes twice, and whose groundbreaking essay, 'When We Dead Awaken: Writing as Re-Vision', first published in 1971, has clearly both influenced Boland's own enquiries and left her unsettled by the American poet's unflinching radicalism. Boland claims that this 'separatist' or 'antitraditional' position tempts the woman poet, 'to disregard the whole poetic past as patriarchal betrayal' (Boland, 1997: 244). This is very far indeed from Rich's careful and generous analysis, in which she consistently stresses the influence canonical men poets had on her, especially in terms of technique, technique which she refers to as the 'asbestos gloves' which allowed her to handle dangerous and difficult (feminist) material (Rich, 1980: 40–1). However, there is no doubt that, especially during the 1970s, there were many feminists who did put forward arguments as crude as Boland's stereotype.

So far then, Boland has argued that both romanticism and separatism (in their debased forms) constrict women poets by limiting their subject matter, though not, *pace* Trilling, by affecting the way they address their subjectivity. But next she moves on to consider the subjective, by examining what she calls the psychosexual arena. Women, she tells us, have enormous problems not necessarily in writing poems, but in thinking of themselves as poets. She refers to what she sees as 'a profound fracture' between the woman poet's 'sense of the obligations of her womanhood and the shadowy demands of her gift' (Boland, 1997: 247). This fracture results in, 'a final reluctance to have the courage of her own experience. All of which adds up to that distance between writing poems and being a poet' (Boland, 1997: 248).

These three points make up the essence of Boland's 'dilemma'. A debased form of romanticism, the 'Romantic Heresy', limits what women can write about or encourages them to unacceptably romanticize and poeticize their experiences. A debased form of feminist separatism encourages women to turn their backs on the literary canon and to write politically correct poetry. And the inherent conflict between being a woman and being a poet makes it difficult for women to grasp the conflicting identities of being both female and a poet with confidence, which in turn affects the authenticity of their writing.

Let's take these points in turn. First, Boland's assertion that 'poetic experience' is a seriously delimited, profoundly gendered exclusion zone for women's experience. Of course she's right that 'appropriate' subject matter in poetry *is* limited: there's no doubt that certain experiences, particularly collective, public experiences, are difficult to render in the post-romantic lyric. And there's no doubt that these areas of exclusion are riven by gender divisions. But poetic development and upheaval has always extended the boundaries of subject matter, and poets at different times have been anxious to include the hitherto excluded in the lyric. Simply in terms of the (male) literary canon, we can witness Wordsworth and Coleridge's experiments with the vernacular and the subjective, Pound and Eliot's incorporation of modern, urban experience into the modernist lyric or Robert Lowell's 'confessional' poems. In other words, whilst I think that

Boland is correct to argue that, especially a decade ago, certain areas of female experience seemed to be 'beyond the pale' poetically, I don't see this as being the heart of the problem, the 'dilemma' that women poets face.

One of the things that's happened over the last decade is that the audience for (women's) poetry has changed. When Boland was writing, men editors, reviewers and poets had an almost exclusive stranglehold over what was published and considered to be acceptable. These (by and large) white male middle-class heterosexual Oxbridge graduates tended to be interested (unsurprisingly) in poetry which reflected their own social experiences. But, as the position of women changed, so did that of men, and there was a fascinating explosion of poems by men about domestic subjects in the 1980s, largely by the so-called 'Martian' school of poets led by Craig Raine and Christopher Reid. Soon, it even became possible for women to write about babies and nappies. And to get published by the poetry establishment. There's no doubt that, despite Fleur Adcock's anxieties about women's poetry being confined to a feminist ghetto, it was women's publishing houses which helped introduce new readers to poetry written by women which, in turn, meant that the established poetry publishers had to catch up or lose out on an increasingly lucrative market.

In other words, I think that Boland overestimated the effect of her 'Romantic Heresy' on women's field of poetic expression. She made the right point – that women's experience was considered to be unpoetic by the male poetry establishment – but for the wrong reasons. Rather than the influence of romanticism, I think we're talking basic social discrimination here: a decade ago women didn't have influential jobs within the publishing industry (though don't think that the women who are important within the books world are necessarily feminist in their intent). Because of the extraordinary social changes which have occurred over the last few decades, the influx of poetry written by women into the commercial market place has meant that the lyric mode has been extended: both in terms of its 'acceptable' subject matter and also in its mood and range. (And as a result, poetry written by men, particularly younger men brought up around feminism,[3] has changed too.)

Second, I also think that feminist prescriptions for acceptable poetry have faded away, simply because feminism itself has become more complex in its analysis. There's no doubt that early feminist thought had its 'Stalinist' impulses. When I got involved with the Women's Movement in the mid-1970s as a teenager, it was feminist 'political correctness', as we'd now call it, which largely contributed to my ceasing to write poetry at all. Political analysis was particularly functionalist and teleological in those days (I was also active on the Left) and, unless something could be actively seen to forward the cause of the oppressed masses, then it was clearly a bour-geois/patriarchal plot designed to trap us all in a state of false conscious-ness. I didn't wear a bra then, either.

This is not to say that (for me at least) feminism has become irrelevant to the practice of writing poetry: quite the opposite. I think of myself as a gendered, historical subject and I hope I have a nuanced, subtle and complex enough understanding of what that means for me not to feel pres-surized into writing 'correct' poetry. Likewise, my many colleagues who write poems which directly or indirectly interrogate notions of gender and subjectivity don't seem to me to labour under an assumption of what this kind of poem should be like – which is evidenced in the astonishing diver-sity of work being produced by women poets writing here and now. Iron-ically, it was the feminist theory developed in the emerging Women's Studies departments and in the Women's Movement itself – which made both Adcock and Boland uneasy at the time – which allowed the separatist impulse to be worked through and transcended.

However, Boland's third point – about the conflict between femininity and being a poet – is to my mind precisely the dilemma of the woman poet, although she doesn't quite probe deeply enough into this issue. What she misses is the implication latent in Trilling's comment that, '*After Wordsworth [poetry's] prevalent subject was the poet's own subjectivity*' (my emphasis). The significance of this shift adds up to far more than Boland's claim for the deleterious impact of the 'romantic' emphasis on poets as being especially sensitive beings.

The dilemma of the woman poet is deeply embedded in the genre of poetry itself, especially in the idea of poetry enshrined in the post-romantic lyric. In other words, the problem goes far deeper than the issue of subject matter, than what women poets can or cannot write about. 'Acceptable' subject matter is constantly changing, being part of the historically shift-ing formal demands and boundaries of what constitutes 'good' poetry, whereas the dilemma of the woman poet is further reaching. Let me put it this way: why have there been so few 'successful' women poets – as com-pared to women novelists – even within a radically revised literary canon? What's the matter with us? This is the thing that bugged me when I started writing. Like all beginner women poets I was highly conscious of learning my craft from men poets, I was conscious of the absence of older women poets. But I was also steeped in the work of women novelists. So what was it about women poets?

The main virtue of Germaine Greer's bloated attack on women poets, *Slip-Shod Sibyls: Recognition, Rejection and the Woman Poet*, is that she asks some difficult questions:

If we ask ourselves why we have no female Blake, for example, we will have to probe deeper, beyond questions of literacy or privilege or patronage or support or even recognition. Homer and Milton were blind; can we claim that being female is a worse handicap than being blind?

(Greer, 1995: xi)

Well, yes, I think we can – simply because if we don't accept that women are peculiarly disadvantaged as poets, then the only other way to account for male poetic pre-eminence is that they're simply superior beings. Whilst it's true that, as Greer implies, 'questions of literacy or privilege or patronage or support or even recognition' can be shown to affect the working lives of all women writers, there is undoubtedly something peculiar about women as poets which transcends these more socially-based forms of discrimination. In other words, there is something about the *form* of lyric poetry which makes it especially difficult for women to write.

Since romanticism, poetry has become virtually synonymous with the lyric, banishing epic or narrative and dramatic poetry to the sidelines. It is the lyric which, historically, has become associated with writing about the self. The American critic, Helen Vendler defines lyric poetry as 'the self's concentration of itself into words'; and James Joyce said that it is 'the form wherein the artist presents his image in immediate relation to himself'. Although of course this self presented in the lyric is a fictional construction, it is a fiction which manifests itself in the fiction of a desiring subject, an 'I' that wants, that is in control (even if only to create the fiction of being without desire or of loss of control). Women, of course, are not traditionally able to take the place of desiring subjects in a patriarchal society: we are the desired objects. And lyric poetry, of course, is the very form in which our status as desired objects has been most fully and most poignantly articulated. Coupled to this, the romantic stress on poetic transcendence and the 'egotistical sublime' is radically at odds with any traditional notion of acceptable feminine identity. With the dominance of romanticism and the post-romantic lyric, the always-irreconcilable roles of woman and poet – the former constructed around self-effacement and constraint, the latter dependent on self-confidence and daring – are even further displaced. The wonder is that any woman dares to write poetry at all. The miracle is that any one who did publish her poetry, certainly in earlier times, survived the violent self-contradictions it provoked.

But what of women poets now? There seem to be so many of us and, everyday, more and more young women poets crop up in publishers' catalogues and appear in anthologies. I think that, for the first time ever, it is becoming possible to be both a woman and a poet. I am lucky to be alive, and writing, now. The reason for this, of course, is feminism and the enormous social revolution that has occurred in the roles of men and women in the west since the post-war period. The contradictions inherent in liberal individualism as to whether women could be individuals – subjects – too, have fractured open to the extent that, in the literary form most available in the west for the interrogation and dramatization of subjectivity, women now have been able to take their place for the very first time as the subjects of lyric verse.

Which is not to say that any of this is easy, or that we can all relax and go home now because the battle has been won. It won't be until we reach that utopia where women and men are social equals as, despite the advantages women have achieved as poets, despite the fact that women can be the subjects of our own poetry, our work is still inflected (and infected) by inequalities and by our objectified subjectivity. Although many of us are enormously privileged in ways our mothers could not even have dreamt of, we still inhabit a patriarchal society. We are not yet fully human. We're living through a period of extraordinary upheaval and transition and those who live through revolutionary times will bear the scars of our historical moment, even if they're invisible to us.

That said, I am encouraged and inspired by the sheer number of women poets now writing and being published. I am encouraged by the fact that the critiques, complaints and anxieties articulated by Eavan Boland, Fleur Adcock and Carol Rumens now sound so dated – for the most positive of reasons in that times have improved unimaginably over the past twelve years. (I can only hope that this small essay will be past its sell-by date so rapidly.) I'm inspired and encouraged by the sheer variety of work being produced in these islands by women poets: comic, satirical, erotic, intellectual, political, lyrical, formal, informal – there seems to be no corner of poetic style that today's women poets feel inhibited about exploring. The woman poet's dilemma may be far off being resolved. But perhaps that dilemma which, in the past, constricted poets to the point of silence, can productively provoke a new and nuanced form of lyric for the next millennium.

Notes

Sarah Maguire has published two collections of poetry, *Spilt Milk* (London: Secker & Warburg, 1991) and *The Invisible Mender* (London: Jonathan Cape, 1997).

1 I'd like to set up a few boundaries before I get stuck in. One, I'm writing exclusively about the literary mainstream, the poetry establishment, page poetry – whatever you want to call it. I'm writing about that zone because it's the one I

inhabit. Two, this zone is confined geographically as well: to Ireland and Britain. Three, you'll notice that I don't name individual women poets (apart from those whose work I'm examining directly). It's a small world. I know all these women. If I mentioned one poet and not another simply in passing that wouldn't be fair.

2 Boland's article, originally published in *Stand*, was reprinted in her collection of essays, *Object Lessons* (1997). As this is by far the more easily accessible text, I've referred to this version throughout.

3 I'm not, of course, implying that men's poetry has taken on a feminist agenda! In fact there's been rather a lot of discussion of a 'laddish' tendency in contemporary British poetry, Simon Armitage and Glyn Maxwell being the most frequently mentioned names in these analyses. What I do think has happened is that men's poetry has become more gender conscious. For reasons of space, I will simply cite the titles of two recent collections to make this point: *Masculinity* by Robert Crawford (London: Jonathan Cape, 1995) and *God's Gift to Women* by Don Paterson (London: Faber & Faber, 1997).

References

ADCOCK, Fleur (1987) editor, *The Faber Book of 20th Century Women's Poetry*, London: Faber.

BOLAND, Eavan (1986–7) 'The woman poet: her dilemma' *Stand*, Winter, pp. 43–9.

—— (1997) *Object Lessons: The Life of the Woman and the Poet in Our Time*, London: Vintage.

GREER, Germaine (1995) *Slip-Shod Sibyls: Recognition, Rejection and the Woman Poet*, London: Viking.

RICH, Adrienne (1980) 'When we dead awaken: writing as re-vision (1971)' in *On Lies, Secrets and Silence: Selected Prose, 1966–1978*, London: Virago, pp. 33–49.

RUMENS, Carol (1985) editor, *Making for the Open: The Chatto Book of Post-Feminist Poetry 1964–1984*, London: Chatto & Windus.

Tara

Mimi Khalvati

FEMINIST REVIEW NO 62, SUMMER 1999, ISSN 0141-7789, PP. 67-77

In November of 1997, my daughter Tara was told she had a rare, con-
genital disorder, affecting her connective tissues. In my poem for her, there
are oblique references to this but, more directly, her diagnosis lay behind
my impulse to celebrate her and her doings, chronicling them as they took
place under my nose. They did so because Tara, looking for a new start,
left her flat, boyfriend, job and stayed with me for a few months, over
Christmas and *Now-Ruz*, the Iranian New Year which falls on the first day
of spring (the day before Mother's Day). During this time, typically, she
was everywhere but at home until finally she moved out and into her new
flat in Brighton. The poem covers this interim time in her life. It also brings
in Tom, Tara's brother – at 23, one year younger – who was then living
with me and Malih, my mother, who lives in London and is a port of call
for visiting relatives.

My wish to write something for Tara coincided with a recent interest in
stanza forms such as *ottava rima*, exemplary in Byron's *Don Juan*. I'm not
that keen on Byron but was drawn to the rather baggy, hotchpotch, holdall
feel of the form, something you can throw things into – anecdote, jokes,
lyric, discursiveness, narrative, you name it. Something rather like the bags
Tara moved in with. So I threw one into the other. And came up with a
stanza, using not the usual three rhymes (ababbcc) but two. This proved
somewhat easier – I could avoid the sudden revving up into the third gear
of the final couplet and, by staying with the *a* rhyme, bring the couplet
back into the body of the stanza. I suppose I had in mind a feminized,
domesticated version of a chronicle – and enjoyed giving the minutiae of
our lives so much space to gad about in.

FEMINIST REVIEW NO 62, SUMMER 1999

Tara

I

She misses her garden. Asks if you can pot
bluebells as I opt against primulas
and answer *no . . . yes, they are lovely but
I only like bluebells in large numbers.*
Woods swim in our eyes. She's got apricot
streaks in her hair now and sunlit, on buses
her eyes go apricot too, like a cartoon
two-tone tiger. She misses Luke, her partner.

I have headaches and eat nut roast I'd never
have made on my own, reliving feasts, roles,
without her I'd never remember. With her,
and now her belongings, a spinning wheel, wools,
boxes and bags of junk friends tease her for,
a dying fig, a thriving mess and pole
of energy we, the quiet ones, mother
and brother are whirled around, they're set astir.

Old dungarees, stuffed animals and live ones
she named, like Adam, goatie, kitty, bear;
flower fairies my hat, a wave of her wand
conjure to cap the toadstool of my hair;
nighties midday sun on a landing runs
back to see halting, see-through on the stairs:
every year of her childhood, little bones
so easily fractured, are in hers, fullgrown.

Given once to me, I gave thanks, but now
offered again what I thought was a one-time
gift I betrayed, chucking out babygros,
bootees, mindlessly committing the crime
that leaves mind's cupboards bare, spurning the rows
of clothes and props I could have used to mime
times love thinks it stores but memory throws
away, lost figures, facts, I'll write what goes.

Pity the girl facing us on a train.
The three of us, on a three-seat and she
bang in the middle of an empty one
opposite. We'd stood there. Reluctantly
she'd moved her legs. We staggered in and then,
before we'd barely sat, out of the very

air came a voice, for her, for everyone:
So why did you apply for this position?

The girl didn't know where to put herself.
My daughter's like that. Talks to strangers, wants
Lillie, her father's dog, to keep her safe.
Takes Terri, her terrapin, tank and all, cross-
country to rig up a home for him, roughs
it in a caravan in Cardiff, pants
upstairs at midnight to keep us up, scoff
icecream, do her stuff, collapse, swan and shoot off.

She's gone off now to Edinburgh. I came
across a line the other day that made me
think of her. And of Tom. Squeezing one last game
out of soap bubbles. Railway arches empty
of travel but for bubbles, some double, some
so large they wobbled with weight, others weeny
as bubbles babies blow, signalling dream
with milk and breath, lips frothy, eyelids gleaming.

So many. Christmas baubles. Christmas stockings.
I love our parent clichés. Yes, when you think
they've gone, don't blink, they're back again. Bringing
not just laundry but baggage to the brink,
old guilts, old sores, old no-win games. Mocking
you with stereotypes, stains, smalls that sink
to the bottom, float to the top and stopping
the rot, tears, hugs, laughter that leaves you rocking.

And it never ends. I'll phone her today.
*I can't hang about waiting for Mum to raise
her head*, she told my Mum, who entered the fray
as if reproach were a baton to seize
and whip to the post in the mothers' relay.
You can't win. But at least we have our clichés.
Shaking our heads as we shrug, pushing away
years of ripostes burning to have their say.

Tom's gone to rehearse. He's been very quiet
these days. It gets on her nerves. Or so he says.
He's right. Honesty's a family trait.
So's jamming the phone. We have two lines and they
converse: one rings, the other immediately
rings back. Sometimes they bicker, sometimes play

and in the silences I get to straighten
cushions, papers, post, keep the whole world waiting.

But not my daughter. Not these days. When things
are bad. And even then we giggle. Hearing
her giggle makes her physical, makes hearing
seeing, seeing feeling, move me as near
to the touch of her as that photo lifting
a bottle to her lips, kingfisher beer
on an Indian beach, another smiling,
hair in her face, a key round her neck, shyly.

Love's in the body. Governs it. Its teat
and tug, ebb and flow. And the body is
the gauge of love, a gauge that can't be cheated,
a language forever fluent in memory's
bones. Have you ever gone white as a sheet,
legs buckling, with a world going to pieces
stuck in your throat? Nowhere but in the meat,
sinew, nerve, can we know how deep love's seated.

Tara was a name I thought I'd invented.
Short for Taraneh. That would sit as well
on an English tongue as a Persian, that went
as well with Tela as with Jane, her middle
name. (Tela, my grandmother's.) It wasn't
till we came back to England that hotels,
laundries, arts groups, goddesses, represented
her to the public, to her puzzlement.

She'll be home tomorrow. With any luck.
Time with her is as fluid as a mood,
expansive as a battered suitcase. Clocks
reverse themselves as easily as childhood
averts disaster, turning hurting back
into healing, a bandage making good
the damage so long as the odds aren't stacked
and hairline cracks no more than greenstick fractures.

This is where childhood ends for most of us:
at the end of a line of slips and falls,
flyaway, gaptoothed, slapstick, dangerous,
after the breaks, apple tree burials,
comes the slow – and how slow it is – slow grievous
realization that our children – call

them kids – are long past that stage, glorious
stage where nothing lasts, time's not merciless.

Which makes them ordinary in our eyes.
Because mortal. Ordinary as Tara,
a common or garden name nowadays.
Like Tom, Ben, Sam, the children of an era.
But there's a bloom on the spirit which, because
it lasts, makes us wonder why our own ever
disappeared. Childlike, an *enthousiasmos*
we marvel at: *she's just the same, remember?*
– though here she is. And our years thought lost, with her.

II

Bluebells are an endangered species. Due to
commercial exploitation. The radio
said so in those drifting island voices you
wake to, half-listening to dream, and only
when you hear bluebells, bluebells dangled two
or three times do you know day's on the go,
Monday, while bluebell woods fall back to view
Sunday's sanctuary. It's true though, true.

So's the baby pigeon story. In Oxford
in the middle of town, waiting to meet
Zeb for lunch – there it is, a baby bird
that fell from somewhere way up at her feet.
It falls again. And as she watches, girds
its loins and marches off, not down the street
but straight into Dillons. Where it is captured,
shopped to the RSPB. Who but Tara'd

do such a thing? So believe what you hear.
It was such a mission . . . Mum's lost the plot . . .
because it was and I have, because Tara,
my unwitting muse, won't stay in the same spot
for two minutes. What am I, chronicler
or scavenger? A magpie with a bon mot
in my beak. An eye to glitter, an ear
to chatter, struck dumb if neither is near me.

Have I crossed some line? Tots, you tell me. Sweet
as you are, you won't. Not the truth. The kernel
and the nub, where the rub is. In the fleet

of omissions. So I won't ask you. Tell
you how I'm spying, capturing you, sheet
after sheet in your presence, absence, while
you toil upstairs on my mailing list, treat
yourself to trips, stay up all hours, don't eat.

And hate coming home late at night like last night
when we both stayed up, swapping tales of nutters
you meet – mine with a butt, wanting a light,
then a whole fag, then change, then, in a mutter
lurched across a bus, asking me to write
his budget; hers, mates mostly, with their clutter
of screens and speakers, crazed computer hermits.
Mad Paul, who stole a friend's koi carp and ate it.

Like him, I thought koi carp were giant goldfish.
Two grand, they're worth, Tara tells me, *it's all
in the markings.* Fleas live on human flesh
for four days, beetles, mimicking termites, pull
their bellies over their heads and in their wish
for perfect tension spiders, liable
to stick to their own silk walkways, accomplish
them on scaffolds eaten to a fine finish.

What odd things you know – the female of fallow
deer is a doe, of red a hind, a dwarf
is not a midget – and she laughs *you're so
funny Mum* and makes me feel it. Half Mum, half
child, protecting and protected, as though
ignorance were dottiness, daft enough
to play with, common knowledge we don't know
is ours an empty patch to romp and grow in.

Like Mother's Day I thought was our New Year,
Now-Ruz, first day of spring. And hence my flowers
first thing. But I was one day out and they were
ahead for once, stripping me of my power
to lay guilt trips. And it was, that day, sheer
March magic to do nothing, not a shower
in sight and Tara, holding forth on nature
on a park wall, making us all feel creaturely.

Oddly enough, termites and goldfish surfaced
again tonight, at Malih's. Swallowed live
they have medicinal properties: laced

with banana, termites help you survive
hepatitis and in Iran they'd chase
those tiny goldfish that were said to hive
off flu germs but were hard to find in those days
with ponds full of fish – *for who*, Malih says,

wants to eat their own goldfish? She's our last
outpost of knowledge. Gathering-post for news
of relatives, once so many, reduced
now to an inner circle, marked by eyebrows
as unmistakeably part of the host
family. Round the table at *Now-Ruz*,
on honeymoon, in transit, holding fast
to fact or fiction, either way they trust it.

And we are her trusty kin. We three, standing
in for the five thousand we should have been.
Tara looks like her. Has been dealt a hand,
in fact, by everybody. Granny Jean.
Her dad, his sister. But like spider strands
only seen when strung with dewdrops, we're seen
in a flicker or flash, profile abandoned
to wind, a jaw, a temple, glimpsed in tandem.

She has ravelled us in. And flung us out
again in gestures scattered over Britain.
And we're recognized perhaps by the doubt
that asks her where she's from, in an Iranian
corner shop she's found near her one-room 'flat'
she's painted yellow, kitted up in Brighton
– now B-RIGHT-ON – or in meat markets flouted
by paintclothes – poxy clubs we're told about.

But what of Tom? Tom who carried the plant
to Malih's. Trundles home her knotted bundles,
leftovers, eked-out feasts. Whose word for want
– *numsum* – plagued us for years, as our pinched fondles
still plague him. Tom with all these women. Bent
to their will, to their cheeks and hair, disgruntled,
compliant, clenching fists to stem live currents –
Tom, our gentle giant, who never meant it.

. . . A thumbnail sketch for you, Tom, who ask me
how my poem's going. While Tara, peering
for new leaves, you above her, she half-masked

by banisters, asks you to lug her weeping
fig to Hove and I, taking you to task
– however I mask it – for interfering
with the sounds in my head, when you're gone, bask
in the silence instead of in your music.

Tom who has finally discovered mornings.
I'm only good in support was his Dad's
keynote, a line from a part he was born for
in Rosencrantz and Guildenstern are Dead.
As a woman I loved him for it. Torn
now between womanhood and motherhood,
what might be a beacon, might be a warning,
it's not for me to say. You know best darling,

both of you do, what to take or reject.
It's when the choice is no choice, blood itself
and time and luck make it for you, select
this gene, that, from their laboratory shelf,
that support comes into its own, erects
an invisible scaffold, spans the gulf
with threads from its own body to connect
opposing bluffs, bridge the voids of neglect.

III

There's bluebells for you I say, *where?* she joins me
at a window propped open by a knife-
sharpener that later falls to join three
plaster frogs and a ladybird. In new leaf,
bluebells at their feet, two enormous trees
lattice the back view of a church. Her new life
will look out on this, this apology
for a garden, this longed-for privacy.

Is the knife-sharpener rusting? Did she meet
its new owner? How, now she's discovered
showers set off the smoke alarm, will she beat
the system? *This is the first time*, I ventured,
you've ever lived on your own. Yes, it's great,
she beamed, proudly, *and the right time*, I added
before she saw me off, her great brown coat,
hood down, hair tied back, exposing a throat

I see for the first time's just like a swan's,
swivelling here, there, now to greet Shrimp, Lisa's
boyfriend, now to browse stalls down North Laines,
craning, failing to find orange tree china;
now thrown back to sun over my sardines,
her pasta, olives, anchovies, two lagers;
and finally gliding past as the train
pulls out, naked as the winds it disdains.

She'll meet Tom tonight, hauling down her suitcase,
her bag, her telephone she hasn't yet
got a line for, rags she hasn't got space for,
show him her folding futon someone threw out
and someone else passing hitched to her place
on his bicycle, the deckchair she'd put
him up on if only the futon base
had a futon to match: her matchbox palace.

He'll admire it the way I did, regaled
by fiery brushwork, orange and red flames
in her hall she calls a hellhole, by tales
of burning toast setting off that same
alarm and engulfing neighbours with bales
of smoke as if to match a colour scheme
planned to kill the disgusting pink of tiles
in a bathroom no-one shares. And he'll smile.

Tell her, as I did, that it really works.
(She's had new keys made. And the old ones, strung
from a pebble with a hole in it, lurk
where she dropped them in the dark, beached among
the very pebbles where long ago Luke
had found the one she nicked, for four years hung
onto and now – why now, here? – lost. It spooks her.)
But no, it wasn't like that, Tom rebukes me.

The paintwork was like flowers. Pebbles poured
into the loose sole of his shoe he later
glued with gold paint, spotted with thumbprint leopard
spots, white-spirited to a glaze, then made her
a gold candle-holder out of a cardboard
box like a pizza box and having stayed
one night on that – *that thing* – *that* – he could hardly
bring himself to utter the deckchair word –

75

bought new shoes in the morning, had a ride
on the carousel – no-one about, rain
drizzling down – and loved the penny arcade.
She didn't want him to leave. I imagine
her frozen – windblown, laughing, her mouth wide
open – in a time frame: forever risen
high on a horse, shouting, screaming asides
to the weather; and Tom below, beside her.

That's one imaginary picture. Reading
Tara through Tom's eyes, him through hers, as if
I were the node through which they cross, misleading
me, putting me right, tracing hieroglyph
arcs in parting gestures. The one receding
as the other draws near, bringing a whiff
of private conversations. And me needing
to draw them out, feed on them as I feed them.

That's one. And there'll be others. Real ones too
like Tara, oiled in lamplight, rosy brown
from one day's sun, knotting these turquoise blue
beads on my wrist, with so much space around
her head now her hair's up I wonder who
could bear a world so welcome. And unfounded
fears rush in and hands wishing they were two
high walls, lift to cup her cheeks, ears, to woo her.

When bad things strike from without, suddenly
the bad things from within seem not to matter.
If you can face a common enemy,
the alliance against it bonds you together.
Ours is no different from anybody
else's, our enemy – time, health, bad weather.
What our genes will make of us. Or what we
will make of them. And no-one wants to see

their child less fortunate. Though Tara's not.
For I never had this courage, spirit, this
bobbing cork of her glee and dumps, this pot
of gold her rainbows jump for, jump and miss
and jump again. Or if I did, have forgotten
– and underestimate – how the sheer bliss
of being alive can be the antidote
to bad weather that wisdom, caution, forfeit.

So, my love, having talked to you or been
in touch without touching you, with a toe
in the past but wading into a keener
sense of the future – for going it solo
has its rewards, an open stretch to wean
ourselves off loneliness – where do I go
from here? Without you, how do I find meaning,
colour, texture? Hear a story beginning –

a voice at the door, climbing up, a live
squealing in my ear? Your burble and bounce,
your *guess what, Mum?* brimming over. Or sieve
that open stretch of stillness for an ounce
of the quicksilver you've supplied and I've
jotted down in secret? Flashes I've pounced
on, others let go, knowing nothing'll give
the whole, the true picture. But you'll forgive me.

You and me both. With our bad records, blotted-
out memories we should have grasped but skimmed,
not taking time to mope, taking joy as read.
So take this as a record, a glancing whim . . .
(Tom rang. You'll never guess. He's shaved his head
and beard. *So what do you look like?* I asked him.
Er . . . like the top of a pencil, he said.)
. . . like his, a whim I followed, you suggested.

Though records hijack what they try to save,
it's a beginning, like you said. Allowing
pain, loss, to penetrate. A time to savour,
time to regret. Sweetheart, I won't wallow,
embarrass you. But when I see you bravely
learning what I'm trying to, when I swallow
my pride, acknowledge things I never gave,
what can I do but owe these debts you waive?

Note

Mimi Khalvati has published three collections of poetry, all with Carcanet Press: *In White Ink* (1991), *Mirrorwork* (1995) and *Entries on Light* (1997). She is a founder member of The Poetry School, which runs writing workshops in the London region.

British Lesbian Poetics:
A Brief Exploration

Liz Yorke

FEMINIST REVIEW NO 62, SUMMER 1999, ISSN 0141-7789, PP. 78–90

Abstract

In a post-feminist, post-lesbian feminist, postmodern or queer world, should lesbian work remain clearly identifiable, even when it refuses to claim lesbian identity as such? Scanning anthologies from the past three decades of lesbian poetry, and focusing particularly on the work of Maureen Duffy, Marge Yeo, Dorothea Smartt, Gillian Spraggs and Carol Ann Duffy, Liz Yorke addresses issues of lesbian visibility, lesbian identification, lesbian desire, and lesbian performativity. How do we identify what constitutes a lesbian poetic in an era when 'lesbian' as an identity is less overtly defended, and many anthologies gloss over lesbian difference in prioritizing a higher order dedication to theme?

Keywords

feminism and literature; cultural studies; lesbian literature; poetry criticism; lesbian poetics

I have on my shelves well-thumbed copies of *Beautiful Barbarians: Lesbian Feminist Poetry* (Mohin, 1986) and *Naming the Waves: Contemporary Lesbian Poetry* (McEwen, 1988) and so anticipated little difficulty in focusing on work emerging from Britain. As I searched for appropriate texts for this article, I found a great deal of information on American lesbian poets, but a paucity on British, especially during the last decade, and this concerned me. I did find many lesbian names I happened to know in collections of women writers, with little or no attention being drawn to their sexual orientation, though the category 'woman' is happily proclaimed on the cover. Has anything more recent, perhaps a collection, been published comparable to that produced by American editor Clare Coss, whose *The Arc of Love: An Anthology of Lesbian Love Poems* (Coss, 1996) declares itself on the cover as 'a tribute to the rich diversity of the lesbian community – a community that continues to thrive in a hostile and chaotic world'? Apparently not. I returned to Lilian Faderman's *Chloe plus Olivia* (Faderman, 1994: 689) to try to make sense of this, and reading this book led me to wonder how far do British lesbian poets now feel themselves to be post lesbian-feminists, or indeed, post-lesbian?

Faderman suggests that

> this younger generation of lesbian authors simply takes for granted lesbian-feminist principles rather than foregrounding them in their work. For example, lesbian love poetry is less likely now to be presented in a political context than it was during the height of lesbian-feminism.
>
> (Faderman, 1994: 689)

Clare Coss, in direct contrast, declares:

> Lesbian poets write about many subjects, not just love and relationships. Many are fiercely political in the cause of justice for all people. They are angry and activist. They care about dignity; they envision a world of liberty, possibility, and decency.
>
> (Coss, 1996: 31)

This statement may perhaps be post lesbian-feminist, but it is certainly not post-political: this led me to wonder how do lesbians present themselves, how do we identify what constitutes a lesbian poetic for the 1990s? This is a large question which I can only begin to ask here, but it is a question worth asking in a postmodern era when an assertion of 'lesbian' as an identity is less confidently defended.

Closely comparable to *The Arc of Love* in its aim to 'include poems that ranged across the whole experience of love', yet very different in its conception and structure is *The Virago Book of Love Poetry* (Mulford, 1990: xiii). Mulford places lesbian and heterosexual poets alongside each other and declares that the book 'ignores boundaries, aiming to demonstrate the affinities and continuities between many kinds of love'. This is a superb collection of writing by a diversity of women but, quietly, I worry. Does this commitment to diversity in the end mean that lesbian difference can comfortably be glossed over, can it yield without loss, to a higher order dedication to theme? Does such a movement depoliticize, fragment, and diffuse/de-fuse lesbian specificities? Emma Perez, in her essay 'Irigaray's Female Symbolic in the Making of a Chicana Lesbian *Sitios y Lenguas* (Sites and Discourses)', has argued that 'If we do not identify ourselves as Chicanas, lesbians, third world people, or simply women, then we commit social and political suicide. Without our identities, we become homogenised and censored' (Perez, 1994: 106). Of course, even within collections of lesbian poetry, diversity and difference between lesbians is now axiomatic – so what am I arguing here? My problem is that lesbians as such simply disappear. I ponder: if this trend were to continue, could searching for my inheritance or my peers as a lesbian writer become incredibly difficult once more? For very different reasons to those of the pre-radical feminist era, but the outcome could be the same. In a post-feminist, post-lesbian feminist, postmodern or queer world, should lesbian work remain clearly identifiable, even when it refuses to claim lesbian 'identity' as such?

But then what does make a lesbian poet? And how does she achieve such identifiable specificity? The copy I found of *Evesong* (Duffy, 1975) for some reason had 'closet library' stamped all over it(!), but her poems spoke out loud and clear. This is 'For Madame Chatte'

> [. . .] Some breasts are erectile
> you say. It may be.
> I can only speak of those
> that are sleepy
> heavy with pale dreams
> awaken to my lips
> pout but with maiden mouths
> are marbled
> hang full as swung
> Parian grapes, as peaches
> espaliered drowsy on a South wall
> that send pleasures about her body
> winged with my breath. . . .
> (Duffy, 1975: 12)

This celebration of these swung breasts is suggestive of a lover's drowsy (post-coital?) appreciation and it seems to me clearly identifies its sexual orientation as lesbian. The poem's sexual political stance is overt, and the reader is invited to share in her delighted adoration, and in so doing flaunts a ripe full-blown sapphic sensuality that is hardly in the closet! Plainly this is a woman writer who adores women, whether she calls herself 'gay' or lesbian, whether or not she prefers to align herself with writers who speak to 'universal' themes, whether or not she wants to see herself as a woman writer, or just as a good writer. But there is no question about the lesbian libidinal intensity of this poem, enabling us to identify 'family' in an instant, whatever 'intention' the writer had in mind.

Lilian Mohin saw her collection as 'creating a new and entire way of perceiving' in which poetry is seen as 'an ideal vehicle for the kind of politics we propose' (Mohin, 1986: introduction). This book, emerging from the Women's Liberation Movement, clearly identified its task as consciousness raising, that is, to use language itself to challenge 'male conceptions of reality', and to do this through writing from 'within the female experience' – including lesbian feminist experience. The orientation of this book gives rise to the related question: if female experience as such must be articulated in order to counter male-centred conceptions dominating current thinking, then is it also necessary for lesbian writers to be identified as such so as to challenge heterocentric modes of thought? Does a writer have to identify herself as lesbian in order that her poem may be included in any definition of a lesbian poetic? How do we formulate what constitutes a lesbian poetic? Marge Yeo, whose work is included in *One Foot on the Mountain*, does not yet in that book identify herself as lesbian. How far can I assume that this extract from the lovely poem 'for loving whole', which explores the very complex attachment to the mother so often found in lesbian writings, speaks with a lesbian voice? Can I count it as a lesbian-oriented poem which may inform a lesbian poetic? Does this writer have to inform us that she is a lesbian to be included here?

> watching her step down slowly
> from the plane, eyes filling up
> (with tears like watermelons,
> i ate unsaid love, ate
> pride, pain) i remember
> everything, salt taste of quarrels
> and tears, body i occupied
> while this flesh grew
> whole, came to seem
> separate
> (Yeo, 1979: 169)

Mother, daughter, sister, lover: the primary intensity of the passion of attachment between mother and daughter are evident here, and inform the deep structure of this tender poem. Luce Irigaray has argued that women's sexual identity finds its deep source in the love for the mother. Since

> the first body they have any dealings with is a woman's body, . . . the first love they share is mother love, it is important to remember that women always stand in an archaic and primal relationship with what is known as homosexuality.
> (Irigaray in Whitford, 1991: 44)

Is this *jouissance,* this primal libidinal intensity, a means to identify a lesbian poetic? Lesbian desire is deeply bound up with desire for the mother in Irigaray's thought. I would suggest that we need to pause here and consider whether this writer should be included as 'family'. The intensity of desire for a woman that can build either after losing a mother through death, or when the mother is unavailable – for whatever reason – certainly can underlie lesbian desire, but is this a sufficient indicator? I think not. The psychogenesis of lesbian desire fascinates me, especially in recognizing that some heterosexual women also experience such desire (perhaps to a lesser degree), but the poem must also be contextualized in time, space and history if we are to begin to identify further modalities of the lesbian voice. The commitment to the personal as political led lesbians towards the

FEMINIST REVIEW NO 62, SUMMER 1999

expression in writing of their self-exploration as a political act. So too, the experiencing of previously suppressed desires became a political act against patriarchal oppression. Female personal experience was to be set against the transcendental and universal value accorded the masculine subject. Publicly declaring a lesbian-feminist stance was to adopt a mode of defiance to the dominant patriarchy as well as to heterosexual cultural norms, but it was also to refuse to detach the symbolic from the material lives of lesbians, and to restore the lesbian – from anomolous stigmatized outsider to centre stage. Caroline Halliday, in the brief biography she offers to identify herself, points here to the very political function of her writing: 'Women as friends, women as lovers, as sisters, workers, mothers; putting women first, this is what feminism really means. It has meant becoming a lesbian and acknowledging that means to be "outside" society' (Halliday, 1979: 54). In reading this radical feminist anthology, I am reminded of what Rosi Braidotti has called 'the power game of legitimation' which she saw as involving the 'creative labour' of feminist reflection to break through 'a logic of exclusion and domination' (Braidotti, 1991: 215–16). Fighting the ideologies, the philosophies, the politics that leave lesbians elsewhere, outside, and absolutely other – in order to inscribe the 'living presence of women in their multiplicity' – is essentially the task of Mohin's collection. But theory moves on: how do we begin to speak as 'lesbian' when each of us possesses such a range of allegiances to different communities, different politics, different modes of expressing who we think we are? By the mid-1980s, Black women were asking hard questions about the dominance of the white women's movement and a new politics of diversity was being forged – lesbian feminist identity politics could no longer contain the multiple tensions within it. This shift makes the formulation of a lesbian poetics utterly contradictory: can there be an identifiable and coherent 'voice' which is clearly discernible in the work of many lesbian writers? Should a lesbian poetic now more simply see its task as being to identify lesbian work in terms of locating within the text an urge to claim community, to find or invent a common culture, or create a sense of belonging among diverse lesbians who are on the 'outside' of heterosexual cultures? Should the critic attempt to discern such voices in the desiring urgencies within the text, as voices longing to belong and which have also to do with the active negotiation and play of power within texts? Perhaps such texts, anxious to speak their libidinal difference and to uphold multiple specificities through revealing to readers what constitutes lesbian identity, are not the whole story. By the 1980s, political lesbianism falters, can no longer contain such a multiplicity of differences within a politically correct frame and so the constraining lesbian identity politics of the 1970s and early 1980s gradually gives way to postmodern performativity. As Carol Ann Duffy was to comment in 1988,

For quite a long time even into this decade we've been allowed certain areas of subject matter, like children, what bastards men are, looms: all these things that appear in late seventies. early eighties women's anthologies. But I haven't got any children and I don't define myself entirely as a woman; I'm not interested in weaving.

(Duffy, 1988: 72)

I turned to Gillian Spraggs' *Love Shook My Senses: Lesbian Love Poems* (1998), as the most recently published collection of lesbian love poems, to try to assess the current position. This book ranges across the centuries and draws on writings from all over the world. Spraggs puts her emphasis on singularity in emphasizing the particular, and stresses the specialness of the bond between lovers

It is sometimes argued that the best love poetry is that which in some sense most inclines towards the universal. I am not persuaded that this is true. I believe that poetry of all kinds is at its finest when it is rooted in the particular. What we respond to in a lover is not, in the end, what she shares with other women, but what is special to her – a look, a gesture, a tone of voice. These are what catch at the heart.

(Spraggs, 1998: xvii)

This turns round earlier attempts to be as inclusive as possible, giving due attention to class and race and other variables of difference; it also takes further the postmodern emphasis on claiming diversity and the recognition of the multiplicity of subjectivity – in promoting an almost Romantic emphasis on specificity. I have spoken of writing poetry as involving 'a willingness to let the unconscious speak' as a consciousness-raising gesture which involves 'bringing the unspoken to speech' (Yorke, 1998: 22; 1991: 190).[1] This lesbian poetry continues to perform the work of re-visionary mythmaking and renaming, which seems to me to partake of the (cultural?) therapeutic process. A delightful poem from this volume, Dorothea Smartt's 'The Passion of Remembrance', identifies the loss of lesbian integrity as an outcome of cultural censorship, for ' "Nice girls" doan sit wid d'legs open/and let the sun stream into them/warming them ouside in':

But y'know which part of me feels confined?
Well!
In this skirt I will not be slow-dancing
with some nice looking sistah
we will not sit face-to-face
her knee my knee
between each other's legs
fingers tracing patterns on the inside of my thigh
making me hold my breath
and count to ten. . . .

FEMINIST REVIEW NO 62, SUMMER 1999

I will not be lying back
vulnerable in surrender in anticipation
of your mouth leaning
on me in me

Nun'na dat!

(Smartt, 1998: 36–7)

This poem gestures towards dignified proprieties that would insist on 'nice-
girl' behaviour, and playfully celebrates the illicit fantastic consummation
of lesbian desires – we are invited vicariously to enjoy with the poet her
generous chuckling spirit of subversion which knows that this lesbian at
least has already partaken of the forbidden! Clearly there are some delights
to be gleaned from censure! It is clear too that this voice is discernibly
lesbian in that it conveys lesbian particularity, contradicts conventional
systems of morality and provocatively contests orthodox condemnation.
This lesbian's active desire for the other woman is hardly contained since
though she describes what she can't do, she creates for herself an intensely
satisfying fantasy of sexual connection. In an altogether different genre and
lexicon Gillian Spraggs' own 'Riddle Game' begins

It is a tower on a wooded hill.
Below, a secret well seeps elixir.
Unicorns drink there.

It is the crest on a strange creature.
Watch as it rears and stiffens.
The mouth opens slowly, like a rose.

(Spraggs, 1998: 32)

Like all riddles it tests our ingenuity in divining its answer or meaning,
though we don't have too much difficulty here! Or do we? This poem tests
our presumptions – for how might a reader know what sexuality is being
represented here? Decidedly phallic imagery seems coterminous with
female, the one indistinguishable from the other – and images traverse the
difference in a fantastic sexual playtime, thoroughly unsettling our com-
placencies and suggestively invoking clitoris as penis, maleness as incor-
porated within the female. Certainly this poetic would, rather, re-imagine
lesbian sexuality as an all encompassing multiplicity of orgasmic potential.
This multi-sexed poem does seem to celebrate all sexualities but, especi-
ally, seems to participate in the identifiably lesbian bliss suggested by the
title of the collection:

It is the mouthpiece of a deep recorder
mellow in tone, and vibrant.
Touch the hole with your finger: hear the note vary.

It is a ridge of folded rock
over a cave with glistening walls.
There are earthquakes in that country.

(Spraggs, 1998)

The poem, actually written in 1983, offers a familiar ecstacy as well as
enacting a recognizable re-visionary strategy – and yet is far from the con-
ceptualizations of contemporary lesbian feminist politics. To borrow Eliz-
abeth Grosz's terms for my own purposes, should I then conceive of 'the
lesbian voice' or 'a lesbian poetic' as always transgressive of established
systems; as marked by its celebration of desire (what- or whoever it ges-
tures towards!) as exploring what may be considered 'taboo' – as well as
demonstrating an authorial desire to represent the 'complexities, ambigu-
ities, and vulnerabilities that can and should be used to strategically discern
[and to refigure] significant sites of contestation?' (Grosz, 1994: 69, my
insert). But how far does other lesbian work support this suggestion? I have
to turn to the work of Carol Ann Duffy to press further my thoughts on
what constitutes a lesbian poetic. I choose Duffy's work in particular for
in her later work she daringly experiments with inhabiting the disturbing
frame of the other. Her earlier poems do embrace the lesbian poetics I have
identified as lesbian feminist. In 'The Way my Mother Speaks' the 'green
erotic pond' of the mother–daughter relation is explored (Duffy, 1994: 88).
In 'Girlfriends' the lovers entwine, bodies connect, desire has its supreme
moments:

That hot September night, we slept in a single bed,
naked, and on our frail bodies the sweat
cooled and renewed itself. I reached out my arms
and you, hands on my breasts, kissed me. Evening of
amber.

(Duffy, 1994: 85)

This poem is marked by its use of poetry to give voice to actual lesbian
experience, its placing of the lesbian lovers at the centre, its affirmation of
a marginalized lesbian identity, its joyful celebration of the consummation
of lesbian desire. However, in her later poems, Duffy will actively decen-
tre identity, refuse the universalizing and romanticizing tendency inherent
in earlier lesbian feminist approaches and refuse to refigure, or reframe or
even strategically contest, cultural expectations and codes. These later
poems characteristically refuse *jouissance*, refuse to imagine desire's con-
summation, even to imagine lesbian desire. In many poems she seems to
invite her readers to transport themselves via a kind of cathartic identifi-
cation, having partly to do with spectacle, yet also having to do with
empathically partaking of creature suffering. She asks of her readers that

FEMINIST REVIEW NO 62, SUMMER 1999

we enter into that which is not contained within culture. We explore that which, in conventional thought, constitutes the despised, or 'sad' or 'sexually deviant' other. In 'Away and See', she invites us to attend to 'the flipside of night', to see who it is that is waiting there: 'let in the new, the vivid,/horror and pity, passion, the stranger holding the/future. Ask him his name' (Duffy, 1994: 107). 'Liar', 'Boy', 'Fraud', 'Stafford Afternoons', 'The Biographer' and, more recently, 'Mrs Lazarus', 'Mrs Tiresias' and other poems from *The World's Wife*, included in the same volume, all press this poetic into being and exemplify this refusal to marginalize the other. In embracing the *not me* so intelligently, Duffy's work actively refuses the politically correct stance, the shoulds and oughts and musts of lesbian moral imperatives and invites her readers to engage directly with that which is not contained within the culture – whether of lesbian activism, or of conventional heterosexual morality. 'Boy', for example, sympathetically explores the pathos of the situation of a man who has experienced being given a bath by an older woman, who now engages in the eroticized sexual fantasy of 'being small':

There was an older woman
who gave me a bath. She was joking of course,
but I wasn't. I said *Mummy* to her. Off-guard.

Now it's a question of getting the wording right
for the Lonely Hearts verse. There must be someone
out there who's kind to boys. Even if they grew.
(Duffy, 1994: 78)

Desire reaches out, having limited hope of finding satisfaction. And the poet's words break through any discomfort at encountering this unusual sexual predilection towards a deeper understanding of the otherness of this sexual difference. The poet enters into the frame of this particular other's point of view and, without judging or blaming, allows the reader to experience the reality of this 'I' for themselves. This poetic invites a complex expansion of acceptance, rather than simplistic knee-jerk condemnation. What fires this troubled imagination? Indeed, what experiences, insecurities, longings, or practices inform a wide range of heterosexual, lesbian or other desires? These poems mark a profound shift towards a freer analysis of many differing sexualities, moving beyond the preoccupations of perhaps a more limited lesbian vision towards a post-lesbian poetics. In the astonishing poem, 'Mrs Tiresias', Duffy examines the process of *becoming the other*, but from the perspective of the conventionally othered, the wife: 'he went out for his walk a man/ and came home female' (Duffy, 1994: 137–40). Despite the shock, she supports this shapeshifting transition and ironically witnesses his difficulties in a new female breasted body:

Then he started his period.
One week in bed.
Two doctors in.
Three painkillers four times a day.

And later
a letter
to the powers-that-be
demanding full paid menstrual leave twelve weeks per
year . . .

Tiresias as female never quite gets being a female right, and this poem
enjoys its mocking feminist edge. The elaborate play between codes allows
for several political volleys, male and female versions of *what femaleness
is* compete and this fascinating site of contestation is amusingly rehearsed.
'Trained up' in the arts of being female by Mrs Tiresias, s/he must learn
the female role, just as s/he learns heterosexist homophobia from the
culture: '*Don't kiss me in public . . . I don't want people getting the wrong
idea.*' This male-to-female 'other' enters the conventionally feminine all
too readily, buying in to a male-centred heterosexuality without question
'entering glitzy restaurants/on the arms of powerful men'. Yet, despite this
extreme femininity, he does not convince the 'real' woman – he remains
'he' to his ex-wife. In a further sexual shift, the former wife's new lesbian
lover asks '*How do you do*' and we know, in that second, that he does not
'do' being female at all convincingly. This is true however he identifies
himself, however he paints his nails and however he endeavours to *speak
as a woman*. His best efforts fail abysmally. His (female) heterosexuality
is in a sense interrogated from within and found wanting. For this male at
least, 'she' is inhabitable only in the most limited culturally determined
fashion. And how is her lesbian lover any different from him? Both paint
their nails, both wear sparkling rings, both trangress and make queer all
these shifts of sexuality – the poet leaves us with many unanswered ques-
tions. However, the poem also sets up an opportunity to realize the move-
ments between male and female, sex and gender, heterosex, and lesbian
sex, in a fluid chain of metamorphic shifts from the one to the other, setting
desire – and its thwarting – teasingly into play.

The effect of this poetic in which imaginary displacements endlessly shift,
and power is repeatedly scrutinized, is profoundly disquieting: whether
approached by a male or female reader, who can with equanimity imagine
'Queen Kong' holding her 'man' so tenderly?

. . . He'd sit, cross-legged, near my ear
for hours; his plaintive, lost tunes making me cry.

When he died, I held him all night, shaking him

FEMINIST REVIEW NO 62, SUMMER 1999

like a doll, licking his face, breast, soles of his feet,
his little rod . . .

(Duffy, 1994: 143–6)

This constitutes a re-examination of heterosexuality (and perhaps of female empowerment!) in which outrageous reversals and dangerous confrontations with the fearful other form at least a part of this challenging poetic. Here in 'Queen Kong', Duffy seems to me to have ventured right inside the male fear of death at the hands of an all powerful female: he meets his end throttled in her grasp, and is ultimately overwhelmed by her poisoned and all-encompassing love. Female power emerges rampant and untamed: the other is set loose upon the world.

My exploration here is all too brief, and space constraints prevent a wider consideration of other important lesbian poets – I would like here to express my regret that I have left out from this tentative exploration of contemporary British lesbian poetics such illustrious names as U.A. Fanthorpe, Maureen Duffy, Mary Dorcey, Jackie Kay, Suniti Namjoshi, Gillian Hanscombe, Patience Agbabi. Nor do I consider my argument fully articulated, especially as far as queer theory is concerned – that will need a book length exposition! My aim here is merely to ask a few questions and to stimulate debate – to stir the pot – and to hope that others will join with me in applauding this continuing tradition, and the many excellent poets contributing to it, by producing further British lesbian collections to delight and challenge readers, unsettling our complacencies over and over again.

Acknowledgements

I am most grateful to Gill Spraggs and Dorothea Smartt for permission to reproduce extracts from their poetry in this paper. Attempts have been made to contact the copyright holders of poetry by Maureen Duffy, Marge Yeo and Carol Ann Duffy without success; they are invited to contact *Feminist Review* for due acknowledgement.

Notes

Liz Yorke is Senior Counsellor at Nottingham Trent University. She has for some years negotiated the divide between research into women's poetry and psychanalysis, and being in practice as a psychotherapist. She taught Women's Writing at Manchester Metropolitan University for ten years and was very much a part of their Women's Studies MA team.

1 Liz Yorke (1998) *Adrienne Rich: Passion, Politics and the Body* (London: Sage Publications) p. 22, and (1991) *Impertinent Voices: Subversive Strategies in Contemporary Women's Writing* (New York and London: Routledge) p. 190. Adrienne Rich coined the term 'Re-vision' as 'the act of looking back, of seeing with fresh eyes, of entering an old text from a new critical direction' (Adrienne Rich, 'When We Dead Awaken: Writing as Re-Vision', in (1980) *On Lies, Secrets and Silence: Selected Prose 1966–1978* (London: Virago) pp. 33–49, p. 35). I borrowed from Rich's quotation to coin the phrase *re-visionary myth-making*, which seemed to me to be more close to Rich's conceptualization than Alicia Ostriker's term 'revisionist mythmaking', which could be confused with evolutionary socialist or Marxist modifications of an earlier theory.

References

BRAIDOTTI, Rosie (1991) *Patterns of Dissonance: A Study of Women in Contemporary Philosophy*, Cambridge: Polity Press.

COSS, Claire (1996) editor, *The Arc of Love: An Anthology of Lesbian Love Poems*, New York: Scribner.

DOAN, Laura (1994) editor, *The Lesbian Postmodern*, New York: Columbia University Press.

DUFFY, Carol Ann (1988) Interview with Andrew McAllister, *Bete Noire*, No. 6 (Winter edition).

—— (1994) *Selected Poems*, Harmondsworth: Penguin Books.

DUFFY, Maureen (1975) *Evesong*, London: Sappho Publications.

FADERMAN, Lillian (1994) *Chloe Plus Olivia: An Anthology of Lesbian Literature from the Seventeenth Century to the Present*, Harmondsworth: Penguin.

GROSZ, Elizabeth (1994) 'Refiguring lesbian desire' in **DOAN** (1994), pp. 67–84.

HALLIDAY, Caroline (1979) biographical note in **MOHIN** (1979).

IRIGARAY, Luce (1981) 'The bodily encounter with the mother' in **WHITFORD** (1991), pp. 34–46.

McEWEN, Christian (1988) editor, *Naming the Waves: Contemporary Lesbian Poetry*, London: Virago.

MOHIN, Lilian (1979) editor, *One Foot on the Mountain: An Anthology of British Feminist Poetry 1969–1979*, London: Onlywomen Press.

—— (1986) editor, *Beautiful Barbarians: Lesbian Feminist Poetry*, London: Onlywomen Press.

MULFORD, Wendy (1990) editor, *The Virago Book of Love Poetry*, London: Virago Press.

PEREZ, Emma (1994) 'Irigaray's female symbolic in the making of chicana lesbian *sitios y lenguas* (sites and discourses)', in **DOAN** (1994), pp. 104–17.

SMARTT, Dorothea (1991) 'The passion of remembrance', in **SPRAGGS** (1998).

SPRAGGS, Gillian (1998) editor, *love shook my senses: Lesbian Love Poems*, London: The Women's Press.

WHITFORD, Margaret (1991) editor, *The Irigaray Reader: Luce Irigaray*, Oxford: Basil Blackwell.

YEO, Marge (1979) 'for loving whole', in **MOHIN** (1979).

YORKE, Liz (1991) *Impertinent Voices: Subversive Strategies in Contemporary Women's Writing*, New York and London: Routledge.

—— (1998) *Adrienne Rich: Passion, Politics and the Body*, London: Sage.

Inn-Between

Karen Kuehne Annesen

FEMINIST REVIEW NO 62, SUMMER 1999, ISSN 0141-7789, PP. 91

In the kitchen Dolce crisps chicken for twenty
in cast iron pans. My first taste of plantains
fried was here, it seems just nights ago,
and even now I can feel them hot
and soft at the back of my throat.
In the hallway Joanne beats back at shadows,
bleaches black and white tiles nearly grey.
Downstairs Gladys works hard at teaching young mothers
childcare while one then two of her children dies inside her.
I make the hostel a home painting walls cranberry and cornflower.
No amount of colour alters Jane's pale stare.
With high heeled shoes
he drove tiny holes in every inch
of her body until she leaked her way here.

Note

Karen Kuehne Annesen was born in America in 1964, but has lived, worked and studied in England and Wales for the past eight years. She works with homeless and disadvantaged women. Her poem, 'Inn-Between' was written while on a writing fellowship at Hawthornden Castle in 1997.

Alcyone and Ceyx

Helen Farish

FEMINIST REVIEW NO 62, SUMMER 1999, ISSN 0141-7789, PP. 92–93

It was the smell of your leather jacket.
When you left the room I would inhale it
surreptitiously in case slave girls
sniffed the scent of my lust.
Doing it I felt I'd been caught
with my legs wide apart and you
hard as my fist of desire.

We had nowhere to go.
The plains of Thessaly exposed us,
served us up on a platter.
The King said how could his daughter
marry someone with a motorbike,
who smoked, who wore ear-rings.
But I could not be persuaded otherwise,
not even by the poets.

When we married I was radiant,
olive oil silking my skin.
I longed to let my hands loose on you,
to smell your foreign country.
Looking back I never really knew
if you felt like I did.
At times there was something about you
as implacable as a flat sea.
But I sang love and wrote it
and left it trailing in the sky.

There was no warning.
I didn't know Zeus had noticed.
You became a diver, me a halcyon.
I was glad each time the sea
wrecked my nest,

glad to watch the waves
unstitch my home-making.
It was never what I wanted.
Zeus knew and disapproved;
for the seven crucial days
midwinter he stilled the sea.

I hate the sky and the water.
My longing for the plains of Thessaly
crushes me like a smell
between the fingers of my memory.
That and your leather jacket
and my dress pressed tight against me
by the wind speeding past.

Note

Helen Farish has had poems published in various magazines including *P.N. Review*, *Stand*, *London Magazine*, *The Honest Ulsterman*, *Rialto*, *Staple*, *Outposts* and *Writing Women*. She was included in the 1998 Arvon Competition Anthology, *The Ring of Words*, and will appear in *The Nerve*, a Virago anthology of new writing. In 1997 she was awarded a Hawthornden Fellowship.

Provisional pleasures:
the challenge of contemporary experimental women poets

Harriet Tarlo

FEMINIST REVIEW NO 62, SUMMER 1999, ISSN 0141-7789, PP. 94–112

Abstract

This article is an introduction to contemporary experimental poetry by women. It considers the reasons for the resistance to such work in this country. It refutes arguments made against it, for example that avant-garde writing is elitist or not related to women's experience. It further suggests why this writing, in particular in its complex engagement with issues of language, subjectivity and gender, should in fact be of great interest to the woman/feminist reader. In particular, it suggests parallels between the concerns of this work and those of feminist poststructuralism. Above all, throughout the piece, it attempts to introduce the 'provisional pleasures' of the contemporary avant-garde to the reader, introducing, quoting and providing multiple interpretations of the work of several diverse writers in this tradition. It aims to provide a sense of the linguistic and formal innovations of these writings, alongside a sense of their relevance to questions of female subjectivity and of women's relationship to the dominant discourses of our time.

Keywords

women; poetry; language/form; provisionality; experimental; poststructuralist feminism

We live in an age of commodification and packaging, in which even our art is served up to us pre-packaged – in this case, our poetry, which we receive anthologized, thematized, or in bite size chunks on the radio. It is not so much this that we should object to, but the fact that these media (books, radio, television, even mainstream poetry venues) all too often like to play safe, so we see the same names in women's poetry, tried and tested, again and again. Another characteristic of our time is the fear of difficulty, the dislike of anything that might require time and applied concentration to enjoy. The image is often preferred to the word. This mitigates against poetry which makes creative use of the page and in favour of poetry which we can access at a single live reading. This essay attempts to convince you that contemporary poetry by women which we can variously label 'avant-garde', 'experimental' 'innovative' or 'postmodern' is worth you, the woman/feminist reader, exploring.[1]

So, temporarily shelving the ideological arguments *against* the experimental, who are these poets and why *should* we read them? Here is a by no means all-inclusive list of established poets in this tradition: in the UK, Caroline Bergvall, Helen Kidd, Geraldine Monk, Wendy Mulford, Maggie O'Sullivan, Frances Presley, Elaine Randell, Carlyle Reedy, Denise Riley and Fiona Templeton; in Ireland, Catherine Walsh; in the US, Rae Armantrout, Rachel Blau DuPlessis, Kathleen Fraser, Barbara Guest, Lynn Hejinian, Fanny Howe, Susan Howe, Karen Mac Cormack, Alice Notley, Leslie Scalapino and Rosmarie Waldrop and, in French Canada, Nicole Brossard. Here then are the names of over twenty poets, most of whom you may well not have heard of, and yet all of whom are writers with a substantial body of work to their names. In the US, where the modernist tradition was kept alive through the mid-century by the popularity of groups like the Black Mountain Poets and the Beat Poets, their work is more widely known and published. Here it still thrives, though with a smaller readership, thanks to the work of small presses like Equipage, etruscan books, Galloping Dog Press, North and South, Oasis Books, the Other Press, Pig Press, Reality Street Editions, rem press and words worth books. These publishers, mainly writers themselves, are committed to lists of exciting new material, with little care for profit. In particular, for women readers, Reality Street Editions' recent anthology, *Out of Everywhere: Linguistically Innovative Poetry by Women in North America and the U.K.*, edited by Maggie O'Sullivan, is a good introduction to some of this work. In addition, new women poets, like Beth Anderson, Jennifer Moxley and Karlien van den Beukel, are appearing through the efforts of the newly formed rem press which is particularly concerned with publishing women's writing. Obviously the work of the poets I have mentioned here is diverse, with greater or lesser emphasis on, for example, lyric structure or performance, and individuals differ as to their commitment to feminism.[2] Yet there are elements we can identify in common in this group. I want briefly to outline these, whilst asking what the woman reader specifically can find here?

What this work shares above all is provisionality, a refusal to tell a simple story or resolve into a single meaning, and its clearly related exploration of and experimentation with language. This returns me to the issue of difficulty, because it is here that mainstream culture and feminist culture have had their arguments with the experimental or avant-garde. Difficulty, or I would prefer to say difference in form, has been seen as exclusive rather than inclusive, as elitist and inaccessible to the woman in the street. A recent article in the *Guardian* on the French feminist theorist and novelist,

FEMINIST REVIEW NO 62, SUMMER 1999

Hélène Cixous, sums up these views succinctly. Whilst the piece did briefly outline Cixous's work on the phallocentricity of language, its title, 'A bit of the Other: Has French feminist philosopher Hélène Cixous got anything comprehensible to say?' and its description of Cixous's writing as 'very difficult, frankly forbidding' though 'if you're in the mood ... quite delightful' culminate in a question which clearly sums up the attitude of the author: 'isn't Cixous's path to female liberation rather too, well, poncey and elitist?' (Jeffries, 1997: 4). Jeffries suggests that 'direct action' feminists must surely share this view and, to an extent, he is right. Editors of feminist or 'women's poetry' publications have tended to exclude the poets I am discussing here. As Marjorie Perloff notes in her essay, 'Canon and Loaded Gun: Feminist Poetics and the Avant-Garde', women's poetry defines itself ideologically, scrupulously including writing of differing cultural and ideological concerns, but excluding writers whose predominant concerns are with poetic form (Perloff, 1990: 35–6).

I would like to mobilize two arguments against the charge of elitism that lies at the back of much of this. First, it smacks to me of old-fashioned paternalism and second, it ignores the fact that radical experiment in art can in fact be seen as radically democratic. *No one* has the reading tools already intact with which to tackle this kind of work. Everyone must start from scratch. The reader is invited in to make their own sense, to have their own experience, within the space this work creates.[3] I find this to be true when confronting English students, trained to read conventional literature, with this work. At the start of a session they will be non-plussed at how to deal with this poetry. By the end, once encouraged to realize that they are not being told what to think here and that they do not have to find the same or single meanings, they are often liberated and exhilarated by the creative possibilities of entering such a space. Reading then becomes a creative rather than a passive experience, as it might be with either a Victorian or a Mills and Boon novel. Both of these are established genres which we know how to read, or not, according to our education and experience. A poem like Carlyle Reedy's 'Indigo' immediately explodes this pre-training:

```
              Green       Snake-like        Goddess
Home of orange  Peony explosions      Pure serious
Hairs arranged
Expressionless          To be paired      To be   flow
             as grow old when young to be
young while old,      mossforest green      close to breasts
          in ribbon shoots   a child   plain
              queen    witch
                a bird            real   in a leaf
```

```
            seer
daughter    of a snake where root strangles    butterflies
white

COLOUR
like a cut              like a scar
```
(Reedy in O'Sullivan, 1996: 151)

The first question we ask is whether to read from left or right or in three columns running down the page, or even whether to read more randomly, from the centre outwards, for example. From the start then we, as readers, have a part in creating the poem. The language too is highly evocative, but ultimately irresolvable. It suggests various reading contexts, such as the mythological, the pastoral, the psychoanalytical and, through the images of women mentioned, the feminist or gendered reading which might easily focus on the development of a girl child from youth to age. Yet no reading of this poem can dominate – and equally several can co-exist, refusing the attempt to simplify complex areas of human culture. At the same time the energy of the poem, the sense of words hurled at the page which we often find in writers like Reedy and Maggie O'Sullivan, provides its own excitement at the level of the arrangement of words and space.

Whilst some poems by these writers appear *more* unconventional than this in appearance (such as Susan Howe's lines printed over and across each other at all angles on the page and Caroline Bergvall's use of graphics) and others *less* so, the possibility of multiple readings persists in all writings. Here, for example, is one of the deceptively short and simple poems of Fanny Howe from her book, *O'Clock*. The book charts this American writer's visit to Ireland and England, and Howe has indicated its concern with time and place (or 'Where is when' and 'When is where', p. 69) by entitling each poem with a date or time:

19: 54

She beetles the sheets with screams.
She puts hair and dying together.
She keeps washing – combing – drying.
She is dwarfed and oppressed by reason.
A she even smaller than a me.
The child Mary? No. A banshee.
(Howe, 1995: 49)

Here Howe plays with simple diction and sentence structure to flummox our linguistic expectations. We expect the word 'dying' for instance to read 'drying', when put with 'hair'. There's wry humour, yet an unease too, when we see our mistake. The structure of the piece suggests a riddle but

FEMINIST REVIEW NO 62, SUMMER 1999

the question, who is 'she'?, remains mysterious. 'She' appears to be marginalized in a domestic yet desperate ('sheets with screams') scene. In the context of this book, which makes reference to Catholicism, 'Mary' suggests the biblical Mary, but the word 'banshee' suggests a traditional Irish supernatural female spirit, an alternative 'she' image. Yet could ban/shee also suggest a banned she, even one who is in some sense 'dying'? We can read the poem then as about images open to women and forces ranged against them (social roles, masculine reason) or as about a dying woman (the banshee wails outside a house where someone is going to die). Perhaps ultimately there is no 'she' or only a dying 'she' (the banshee herself, an old fading image) available to us as women, and this is what the poem ultimately suggests in its lack of resolution, its inconclusive riddling.

Poems like Howe's make us pay attention and make connections, not least with the other ninety-odd small poems in this collection. The interconnectedness of the poems in this text is common to many of these writers whose work mitigates against the notion of the individual perfect work of art, the Keatsian Grecian Urn idea of poetry. Rachel Blau DuPlessis for instance now calls her endlessly inter-related poems, 'drafts', emphasizing their provisionality, and numbering them from one to thirty-eight (so far) stretching across book boundaries. It is hard to quote from such writers whose work never resolves itself into bite size soundbites. As Wendy Mulford found, attempting a similar introductory essay: 'It's almost impossible to end any of these extracts, the fabric is ravelled so tightly, pull one thread and you keep on pulling until nothing/everything goes' (Mulford, 1990: 270).[4] All of this is demanding, not difficult, just *demanding*, but it points also to the absorbing integrity of the work's provisionality.

This provisionality is in turn related to one of its effects and obsessions: the destabilization of the notion of poetic authority (the idea that the poet is a truth-teller who should be listened to). Alongside this, many poets question *identity* itself, or what poststructuralist critics have called subjectivity, a word which suggests a self which is 'subject to' the forces of culture, in particular language and gender. Much critical ink has been spilt in recent years over this question of gender identity, from the theories of 'French feminists' (Hélène Cixous and Luce Irigaray) to Judith Butler whose controversial *Gender Trouble* insisted so powerfully on the constructed nature of gender. Such concerns are reflected in these poetries, although only some of it engages directly with poststructuralist theory, for the question of what we are as women (a biological fact? a cultural construction?, a sex or a gender?, or both?) has become central to the thinking of many feminists this century.

The ever-increasing popularity of women novelists like Virginia Woolf,

Angela Carter and Jeanette Winterson is testimony to the interest of the reading woman in questions such as these *and* to an acceptance that traditional forms are best abandoned to think untraditional thoughts, i.e. to think about women. It is strange that the poetry which, to my mind, best explores these issues is still so little known in this country. Just as Woolf is evident ancestor of Winterson, so the poets I am discussing today draw on the tradition of key female modernists like Gertrude Stein, Mina Loy, Marianne Moore, H.D. and Lorine Niedecker. All these poets are marginalized to varying degrees in this country where the average student or interested reader in search of modernist giants is far more likely to encounter T.S. Eliot or Ezra Pound. Publishers of women's writing and, to a lesser degree, readers, quick enough to reclaim women novelists of all traditions, have neglected women's poetry. In particular, influenced by the conservative tastes in poetry which have dominated in this country for several decades, they have neglected the experimental tradition. Whole areas of women's writing remain to explore.

I have no desire to create new hierarchies and canons reminiscent of the male-dominated academy, but it seems to me that in an era concerned with complex debates over competing identities, a woman's poetry which asks 'who am I? what am I? as a woman?', as experimental poetry so often does, should be at least as widely read as one which is based on identity politics and which is more likely to say, 'here I am, listen to me, as a woman!' Rachel Blau DuPlessis's work is one of the most ambitious in its attempt to do the former, to explore the question of female subjectivity.[5] Her poetry remains acutely aware of the 'rose-pink/ border' of the female condition from babyhood onwards ('Writing', DuPlessis 1987: 62), the cultural constraint and assimilated femininity of the 'quire of girl bound in, bond in, for pink' ('Draft 2: She', 1987: 103). These images from her book *Tabula Rosa* connote foot-binding, baby-binding and book(or quire)-binding alongside the infamous pink for girls, and she connects these images with the blank page (or tabula rasa) of women's writing which has not been seen to exist over the centuries.

DuPlessis is a writer who explicitly engages with poststructuralist feminist theory. Her draft, 'She', examines the position of the female pronoun in our language and culture, whilst in 'Me' she seeks a new female self, suggestive of Julia Kristeva's theory of the 'subject-in-process', or series of 'selving[s]'[6] as opposed to singular self. This pluralized notion of selfhood might perhaps escape encapsulation, perpetually rejecting imposed models of femininity:

Lucid cool green twi-day (say) a struggle
between different

voices competing   don't use that, meaning
that model   that word   to identify
things that   this   isn't it   isn't my   voice

it?

('Me', DuPlessis, 1991: 23)

In order to access this plural unresolved self, DuPlessis draws on Kristeva's theory that, once she enters language, the female self is bound to the 'Law of the Father'. If she can return to the pre-linguistic *chora* or can even exist on the edge of the semiotic (pre-linguistic) and symbolic (post-language) states, then a new voice might be found, a voice which Hélène Cixous has called that of the 'newly born woman' and developed further into ideas of new kinds of female expression or 'writing the body'. The draft 'Me' seems to return to this moment of language acquisition when the girl-child exists in a state of resistance to definition as a single separate 'she':

The big-mouth
bears came chasing me and made me
dash all dark–
far run of little me – and that started
some me screaming *of*
me, a tuneful tidal wave
of much engulfing light.

Do ray me
far so large.

The lines – of green, of pebbled loose –
a fall and scatter near, there mark their move.

Earth star
moon jelly
wobble in waters which
will sting, or sing
you, will

sing already full of voices –
polyphonous voy-
sizz – scissors that sharp
and flat line salt tide
signs:

many;

('Me', 1991: 24)

Here is a moment of Kristevan *jouissance* through language-play, but it is also *about jouissance*, a self-conscious examination of Kristevan and French feminist ideas of return to the *chora* and 'writing the body' (see for example the conscious use of theoretical language in 'polyphonous voices' and many 'signs'). Yet DuPlessis never neglects the fact that, in society, this 'Me', the female speaker, is under constant pressure to remain silent. Later in the poem, she takes up an earlier image of the female poet as bird to restate: 'but sometimes stuck,/can't speak or spit what thrush I got' ('Me', 1991: 26). Here she reiterates the powerful sense of forces which stifle the woman's voice and insist the page is blank.

One of the accusations made against French feminism has been that it lacks connection to the 'real life' world of women, to women's experience, a vexed area in feminist literary criticism. The early work of critics like Ellen Moers, Elaine Showalter, Sandra Gilbert and Susan Gubar insisted that feminist critics should attend to specifically female experience in women's work. This tendency in criticism, when combined with the prejudice against difficulty and in favour of accessibility, has led to an emphasis within and without academe on writing that is *obviously* and *accessibly* about women's lives – a prevailing view which mobilizes opinion against women's experimental writing. In fact, the experience of being a woman, including the specifically female, often physical, experience so beloved of the gynocritics, features in many of these writers' work and should not be so easily divorced from an interest in form and language. It does not however present life anecdotally (whether as private or public) nor does it take private experience as its sole subject. Much recent poetry does both.

Neither does this poetry attempt to reduce our experience to understandable, quantifiable, expressible events happening in the external world. Instead, in the tradition of modernism, it frequently attempts to explore what is going on *inside* our minds as well as outside; what is mysterious, inexplicable and silently powerful, be it ideological influence or spiritual event. For, despite its doubts over subjectivity, as Clair Wills has argued, this poetry *is* interested in interiority (and hence private experience), even elements of expressivity, but it recognizes that these can never be representative and are always constructed through the outer public sphere (Wills, 1994: 34–52). 'Experience' is not only after all a series of empirical events, a series of incidents and conversations occurring in workplaces, supermarkets, homes and bus stops, nor does it only consist of specifically female bodily experience, be it lesbian love, or childbirth.

'Not only' – but obviously it does in part, and that is why I want to show here how such important women's experience does make its appearance in this work, belying accusations that it is too elitist, difficult or over-theoretical to be interested in such matters. (Here lurks another piece of dubious binary thinking – that theory and human experience are unrelated). Catherine Walsh has written her experience of motherhood into her work,

FEMINIST REVIEW NO 62, SUMMER 1999

especially her long poem, *Pitch*, which moves between present and past, Spain and Ireland, incorporating issues of nationalism, gender, motherhood and memory into its spacious, shifting structure. Here is a specifically maternal passage:

I write when he's
asleep I write he
doesn't sleep
much anyway

nobody who hasn't done it can
make you feel the exhaustion how
no thing ever starts or is
finished though when you look
occasionally something finishes
there is no gratitude (that)
finish starts making you feel
exhaustion

(Walsh, 1994: 13)

Walsh uses space and repetition powerfully here. The ceaseless round of caring for a baby is written into the round structure, framed by the word 'exhaustion' and spiralling through the repetition of 'finished', 'finishes', 'finish'. The space between the two stanzas plays its usual role of the breathing/thinking space between thoughts, but also conveys to me the blank exhausted state of the new mother.

Nicole Brossard[7] creates and celebrates a utopian lesbian space in her work. Many of her poems in the book *Lovhers* are prefaced with quotations from Monique Wittig, the French lesbian writer whose innovative novels imagine an exclusively lesbian world. Like Walsh, Brossard is exploring specifically female experience, and yet, at the same time, she does not assume a static essential femininity but continually explores the shifting nature of self. As Caroline Bergvall has identified, she achieves this balance by attention to the body: 'She avoids a lurking essentialism while still seeking a stable referent to writing, by expressing identity through the changing subjectivity of physical experience' (Bergvall, 1993: 35). This extract from 'JULY THE SEA' illustrates Brossard's embodiment of the body in (often erotic) relation to self and other:

memory, some words are such
that an embrace conceives
their surfaces/allusions
because my obsession with reading

(with mouths) urges me
toward every discourse
round the generic sap
obsession tied to what questions
the abandon the conquest vulva wave
the tide of desire the keen defeat
of the writing fervent conquest: to read

----

july the sea is the provisional articulation
of pleasure which my sister brigand draws
our points of falling (emergency curves)
when turning the page means:
to follow
our reading binding our intentions like
a thought
issuing from this force *defeated*
inside our heads celebrating the reflex of vertigo
we can conceive anything
(Brossard, 1987: 35–6)[8]

Here we find Brossard's characteristic belief in the power of imagination ('we can conceive anything'), ending extracts which consider body as text and text as body. The sequence as a whole admits a narrative reading of the work as the history of a sexual relationship, in particular the exchange of power and relinquishing of control, yet the relationship and the 'other' are continually read as discourse and as textual process, a turning of the page, so the piece becomes about control in reading and writing. There is a radical flow in Brossard's work achieved in particular by the abandonment of punctuation (except the colon which opens up the text onwards, rather than closing it down) and the consequent double-functioning of words (so 'a thought' can be a simile for 'our reading' *or* can be a thought '*defeated*' which in turn can be '*defeated*' 'inside our heads' *or* inside our heads can refer to the 'vertigo' out of which 'we can conceive anything'). In fact we do not consciously break down the poem like this as we read; instead we have a sense that 'our reading' both binds and releases (in loss of control – 'vertigo'). Yet we also sense that this 'we', this community of women (or lovhers), this sense of self and other, is the only chance for a new imagining.[9] Brossard's radical flow (suggested by the title of the piece, 'july the sea', which pulls time and place into grammatical unity) never fixes definition of 'woman' or women's relationships, yet always celebrates them. Her work should allay the fears of some feminists that working with ideas of an unstable female subject merely reinforces female lack of status and confidence.

I want to return now to further consideration of form and language, for it is the self-conscious attention to text which above all else puts this poetry in the realm of the 'experimental'. This is a writing which in its unusual forms draws attention to the materiality of language: words as things, rather than words read solely for their meanings; words used more as an abstract painter or composer uses paint or notes in music, for their patterning on the page or their sound value. This technique allows for the privileging of silence and space too, for words unusually arranged force the reader to confront the empty space on the page which more conventional poetry marginalizes over to the right-hand side of a block of work, where it has always been and where, hence, we do not notice it. Once again this has feminist implications. The silencing of women has been a concern of feminist criticism, from the image of Shakespeare's sister dying unheard of at the Elephant and Castle in Woolf's *A Room of One's Own* (1929) to Tillie Olsen's catalogue of silences in her 1970s classic of that name.[10] The poetry of these women poets breaks that silence, but is also able to examine and embody silence on the page in work which makes as much use of the blank sheet as the words.[11]

As to the words themselves, we know, from the influential work of critics like Dale Spender and Sara Mills and from current attention to language politics how important language is in circumscribing how we think and what we can say. We have all now probably replaced the word chairman with chair in our workplaces, yet how much do we really think about how language works on and with us? In fact the prejudices displayed in the *Guardian* article mentioned above hold us back from engaging with writing which takes language and its power seriously. In the poetry I am discussing here, language comes under fierce scrutiny, a scrutiny which is political in every sense. Through exposing the associations of words, the aura of words around a word, and, often, by quoting or parodying the language of the culture that surrounds us, this writing explores how language creates us. In work like this by Caroline Bergvall debased phrases, common coinage, cliché, come back to life, demand to be considered:

> What There Is To Learn From the Fortitude Of These Aggressive
> Plants, Keeping A Clear Head Arbitrarily, Hard To Break The
> Paraded Sequence, Easy To Get Lost, Merely East To Give Up :
> Dreams Get Heavier : Reality More Sudden On Bad Days. . . .
> (from 'The Underlip', O'Sullivan, 1996: 206)

and

WEL is an occupation **COME to**
the foreign guided a short round
of observations. Now yo. s.. now
y.. don'. What not assumd .. be
not hr since forver pleased are
we by and large to kindly be
stuck to instructs or what kind
of langu would we othrwise be
left wit.

(Bergvall, 1996: 7)

In the first piece, the 'paraded sequence' of maxims for survival, drawing attention to its pomposity through the capitalized first letters of each word, dances before our eyes, showing up the absurd language we live by. The second piece, which welcomes the reader into the carnivalistic space of Bergvall's book, *Éclat*, wittily (note that 'wit' is the word we are left with at the end) incorporates familiar words and phrases in fragments, thereby announcing its intention to look at language as 'foreign', the language that is 'othr', that we are left with after we deconstruct the words and phrases we use day by day.

Seeing old words in new contexts like this, we are forced to confront our own culture, rather than simply absorbing it by a constant intravenous drip of advertisements, film, pop music, radio and television. In this way, contemporary experimental poetry is in tune with, yet goes beyond, the postmodern irony that characterizes our age – and our assessment of the past too. Frances Presley, in a recent paper, quotes a line wonderfully suggestive of the 1950s from Lyn Hejinian's *My Life*: 'I was sipping Shirley Temples wearing my Mary Janes' (Hejinian, 1987: 19). Presley insists that this line shows more than 'fascination [with] linguistic objects' – it must be read in terms of the gendered construction of identity where '[g]irls are defined by their names, and by the objects those names are attached to' (Presley, 1997: 6).

Denise Riley's poem, '*Lure, 1963*' swirls 1960s pop song lyrics in with party colours and druggy images, creating a vivid picture of the sixties girl:

Navy near-black cut in with lemon, fruity bright lime green.
I roam around around around around acidic yellows, globe
oranges burning, slashed cream, huge scarlet flowing
anemones, barbaric pink singing, radiant weeping When
will I be loved? Flood, drag to papery long brushes

FEMINIST REVIEW NO 62, SUMMER 1999

of deep violet, that's where it is, indigo, oh no, it's in
his kiss. Lime brilliance. Obsessive song. Ink tongues.

The power of the lyrics to infiltrate attitudes is under examination here, but the final lines, almost solely through quotation, also suggest the fakeness of sixties femininity:

Oh yes I'm the great pretender. Red lays a strip of darkest
green on dark. My need is such I pretend too much, I'm
wearing. And you're not listening to a word I say.

(Riley, 1993: 30)

The references to clothes throughout emphasize this 'dressing up', whilst the words, 'I'm wearing', suggest 'wearing thin' or being 'worn out'. The phrase, 'And you're not listening to a word I say' draws attention to the passivity of the girl who is her clothes and is also the sort of direct challenge to the reader that we often find in these writings.

The engagement with language in experimental women's work not only exposes the language of popular culture, but also the philosophical, scientific or historical discourses of the Grand Narratives that have dominated our century.[12] Rosmarie Waldrop's *Lawn of Excluded Middle* is an investigation into the feminine which both uses and diverges from the laws and language of logical philosophy, critiquing both syllogism and binary thinking, often with ironic wit:

Actually I prefer stories with sharp edges cut by blades manufactured with great precision in Solingen, Germany. These I use like a religion to keep me on the straight and narrative which, like computers and gods, admits only yes or no.

(Waldrop, 1993: 65)

The following piece shows how Waldrop's project leads her to examine the relation of the female body to language, time and history, as well as to the 'other' of the masculine:

The silence, which matted my hair like a room with the windows shut too long, filled with your breath. As if you didn't need the weight of words in your lungs to keep your body from dispersing like so many molecules over an empty field. Being a woman and without history, I wanted to explore how the grain of the world runs, hoping for backward and forward, the way sentences breathe even this side of explanation. But you claimed that words absorb all perspective and blot out the view just as certain parts of the body obscure others on the curve of desire. Or again, as the message gets lost in the long run, while we still see the messenger panting, unflagging, through the centuries. I had thought it went the other way round and was surprised as he came out of my mouth in his toga, without even a raincoat. I had to lean far out the window to follow his now unencumbered course, speeding your theory towards a horizon flat and true as a spirit level.

(Waldrop, 1993: 48)

Here the fractured narrative gives us the silence of a woman 'without history', a silence weighed down by the presence of the unnamed other, but with a desire to explore history and culture ('the grain of the world'). Then a spiralling of simile takes over – language is the metaphor for culture, and the body is the metaphor for language – giving way to the riddle of the messenger, another unidentified male other. This messenger metaphor suddenly becomes actualized in the narrative, absurdly, yet grotesquely, emerging from the speaker's mouth in a comic twist. We and she are left with no answers about the 'grain of the world', as she gazes into infinity after the other's 'theory' – or we could read that his 'theory' is spinning out of her belief system, that she rejects here the whole notion of a theoretical, hence logical, explanation. Certainly when we follow the 'logic' of the piece, we find, as we often do in experimental writings, that it is thwarted, just as the female speaker is thwarted here in her quest, to the point where it becomes comically exposed.

Another discourse, other than logic, is questioned here – Waldrop (like many of these writers) critiques the age-old notion that lyric poetry can give us not only beauty, but truth, the answers to the problems of existence and of love. She refuses conventional poetics, injecting other discourses. When she does employ, as here, the art of metaphor, she shows how it pulls the questor further and further away from her desire, entangling her in a linguistic game, finally exposed by literalizing an absurd metaphor and even dressing it in joke historical wear, a toga. This piece can also be read as part of a history of a relationship. It is in a section of the book called 'The Perplexing Habit of Falling' which, in context, suggests both Newton's apple (with echoes of Eve's apple, the cause of the Fall) and the idea of 'falling' in love. As a sequence of 'love poems' (of a sort), these poems explore sexual difference and power relations between the masculine and the feminine. As ever, we can engage with the work on many levels.

It is not just that language and form *are* in themselves political and that this poetry is therefore always in engagement with the status quo. Many experimental women poets deal explicitly with politics and culture on a wide scale, as well as the women's experience I have already mentioned. Here is a further argument against the accusation that this poetry is elitist and irrelevant due to its concern with poetic form. In fact, most of these poets would endorse Maggie O'Sullivan's quotation of Gertrude Stein at the beginning of her powerful poem, 'Another Weather System': 'And each of us in our way are bound to express what the world in which we are living is doing' (O'Sullivan, 1993: 8). Immediate examples which spring to mind are O'Sullivan's own environmental concerns; Frances Presley's *Automatic Cross Stitch* (1995) which is in part 'a walk around the fashion

FEMINIST REVIEW NO 62, SUMMER 1999

industry'; Elaine Randell's *Gut Reaction* (1987), a book arising directly from her work as a social worker, and Alice Notley's 'White Phosphorous' (1992: 402) which focuses on the Vietnam War.[13]

In an essay on 'Homer's Art' which precedes 'White Phosphorous', Notley declares her intention 'to tell a public story' about war, making connections between the Trojan War and the Vietnam War (Notley, 1992: 401). She writes of speaking in a female voice that 'there might be recovered some sense of what mind was like before Homer, before the world went haywire & women were denied participation in the desire & making of it'. 'White Phosphorous' attempts to do this:

> "no magnanimity" "to an enemy" "no feeling for what" "is invisible" "for
> magnanimity" "for what's lost" "to air, in air" "As if nothing
> replaced chivalry, not something" "invisible" "but nothing." "No one
> cared" "what was lost" "with our air" ("All the forms were already"
> "men") ("politics, a man" "philosophy, a man; a building, a" "painting a
> poem, a man" "science, a man") ("Now, we can all" "be men") "This
>
> is what happened." "She is a mother." "This is what happened."
> "Or she could be a lover" "or a sister" "This happened" "Find green air
> green breath" "Later, he tries to become" ("did he become") "air,
> air, as again" "This is what happened. And she's trying" "to breathe"
> ("the mother") "And she's trying to wash" "to wash off" "America"
> "from herself" "But what" "is a mother" "now?" "In America,
>
> everyone is else". . . .
>
> (Notley, 1992: 407)

This passage is framed with a sense of the brutality of warfare, and subsequent trauma of the soldier figure (trying to become air, to dissipate or self-destroy), but within this we have the female relation (mother, lover, sister) who is trapped within a nation whose culture is masculine (politics, painting, science) and hence exclusive of her, but which she can't 'wash off', her son/lover/brother being caught up in the most deadly proof of nationhood, war. The penultimate question, ' "But what" "is a mother" "now?" ', refers to the whole status of the feminine in contemporary America. The repeated quotation marks work to mobilize the reader's mind: who is speaking? do we have many voices here? is there a sense of authenticity, citation from life, confirmed by the repeated line, 'This is what happened' or a sense that we could speak of any 'mother', 'lover' or nation, 'America' – or both? So the poem questions notions of history and witness, even as it engages with them to 'tell a public story'. In these poems then we find no lack of 'real life', even realism, a term Frances Presley has reclaimed in her writing about Elaine Randell. Yet in all this work we also find a preservation of attention to form which helps this poetry to avoid cliché, simplistic politics or cheap exploitation.[14]

I hope I have shown here that the language-games we find in these writers' work function in a serious political and cultural manner, but as the word 'game' suggests, are also playful, carnivalistic, often joyous and humourous, in the spirit of the great modernist experimenter, Gertrude Stein. The '*jouissance*' of being on the edge of nonsense, which Kristeva describes in her *Revolution in Poetic Language* (1984), is not just about psychoanalytic/feminist/semiotic theory, it is also about the excitement of pushing form to its limits, and the excitement of being the reader of work which attempts this. In addition, in range and depth, this is writing which provides a challenge and an inspiration to the woman reader and the feminist reader as great as any other she might find today.

Acknowledgements

I gratefully acknowledge the permission of the poets quoted here to reproduce their work. I should also like to acknowledge the critical work and support of Caroline Bergvall, Rachel Blau DuPlessis, Wendy Mulford and Frances Presley. Rachel Blau DuPlessis poetry books are available from SPD, 1341 Seventh St., Berkeley, CA 94710-1403, USA; spd@ igc.apc.org

Notes

Harriet Tarlo teaches British and American Literature and Creative Writing at Bretton Hall College, University of Leeds. Her research interests are in British and American modernist and contemporary poetry and she has published on H.D., Lorine Niedecker and contemporary experimental poetry.

1 Some of these poets, especially Lyn Hejinian and Susan Howe, are seen as being part of the American 'Language Poetry' movement, but this is not a title that can be applied to the group as a whole, so I shall not use it here.

2 I do not have time here to cover the question which Caroline Bergvall discusses so well elsewhere of why some experimental women writers are resistant to the 'ism' of feminism (see Bergvall, 1993: 30). In a sense this is the reverse side of the coin to the one I *am* exploring, which is what these writers, whether they *call* themselves feminist or not, have to offer the woman/feminist reader.

3 To show this in action, I have attempted to present readings here that are as open as possible, bringing as little prior knowledge to the text as possible.

4 The quote is about extracting from Lyn Hejinian's work, though my point is that it could be said of most of these poets.

5 Duplessis's *The Pink Guitar: Writing as Feminist Practice* (1990) is one of the best available introductions to both this kind of criticism and these experimental forms of writing.

6 DuPlessis's own phrase, from 'Language Acquisition' (1990: 99).

7 Brossard's *La Lettre Aerienne* (1985) (translated as *The Aerial Letter*, 1988), as well as being a lesbian classic, was one of the first books to explore the practice and preoccupations of writing as a feminist in experimental modes.

8 More available to British readers is Brossard's recent *Typhondru* (1997), her first UK publication, available from Reality Street Editions.

9 Brossard's sense of the community of women, the necessity of a feminine 'genre', has much in common with Luce Irigaray's recent work, *je, tu, nous* (1993), which stresses the need for women to establish a female I and You (self and other) to achieve a feminine genre.

10 This is the context out of which Joan Retallack writes her striking meditation on ':RE: THINKING:LITERARY:FEMINISM:', pointing out how that silence still obscures many of the experimental women writers she considers by damning them to obscurity (Retallack, 1994: 345).

11 One of the most striking examples of this is DuPlessis's poem, 'Gap', in which the 'gaps' of lost memory and death are physically represented on the page through blocks of black appearing like negatives of pages (DuPlessis, 1991: 11–15).

12 This is a characteristic of those writers, like Lyn Hejinian and Susan Howe, who are associated with the Language Poetry movement, but we find it also in DuPlessis, Dahlen, Riley and others. It mirrors the feminist unravelling of psychoanalytic and philosophical discourses that we find in Cixous and Clément (esp. 1986) and Irigarary (esp. 1985).

13 The Vietnam War also features in the more autobiographical work, *Mysteries of Small Houses*, some of which has recently been reprinted in *etruscan reader VII* (1997), Notley's first British book in over twenty years.

14 The use of transcription, sometimes modified and sometimes not in, among others, Randell and Presley provides the opportunity for frequently marginalized women to speak through their work.

References

BERGVALL, Caroline (1993) 'No margins to this page: female experimental poets and the legacy of modernism', *Fragmente*, 5, pp. 30–8.
—— (1996) *Éclat*, Sound and Language.

BROSSARD, Nicole (1987) *Lovhers*, trans. Barbara Godard, Montreal (Quebec): Guernica.

—— (1988) *The Aerial Letter*, trans. M. Wildeman, Toronto: The Women's Press.

—— (1997) *Typhondru*, trans. Caroline Bergvall, London and Suffolk: Reality Street Editions.

CIXOUS, Hélène and CLÉMENT, Catherine (1986) *The Newly Born Woman*, trans. Betsy Wing, Manchester: Manchester University Press.

DUPLESSIS, Rachel Blau (1987) *Tabula Rosa*, Elmwood, CT: Potes and Poets Press.

—— (1990) *The Pink Guitar: Writing as Feminist Practice*, London: Routledge.

—— (1991) *Drafts 3–14*, Elmwood, CT: Potes and Poets Press.

—— (1997) *Drafts 15–XXX*, Elmwood, CT: Potes and Poets Press.

HEJINIAN, Lyn (1987) *My Life*, Los Angeles: Sun & Moon Press.

HOWE, Fanny (1995) *O'Clock*, London and Suffolk: Reality Street Editions.

IRIGARAY, Luce (1985) *Speculum of the Other Woman*, trans. Gillian C. Gill, Ithaca, NY: Cornell University Press.

—— (1993) *je, tu, nous: Toward a Culture of Difference*, trans. Alison Martin, New York and London: Routledge.

JEFFRIES, Stuart (1997) 'A bit of the other: has French feminist philosopher Hélène Cixous got anything comprehensible to say?', *Guardian*, 29 October, p. 4.

KRISTEVA, Julia (1984) *Revolution in Poetic Language*, trans. Margaret Waller, New York: Columbia University Press.

MULFORD, Wendy (1990) ' "Curved, odd . . . irregular". A vision of contemporary poetry by women', *Women: A Cultural Review*, Vol.1 No. 3, pp. 261–74.

NOTLEY, Alice and OLIVER, Doug (1992) *The Scarlet Cabinet*, New York: Scarlet Editions.

NOTLEY, Alice, MULFORD, Wendy and CAFFREY, Brian (1997) *etruscan reader VII*, Buckfastleigh, Devon: etruscan books.

OLSEN, Tillie (1980) *Silences*, London: Virago Press.

O'SULLIVAN, Maggie (1993) *In the House of the Shaman*, London and Cambridge: Reality Street Editions.

—— (1996) editor, *Out of Everywhere: Linguistically Innovative Poetry by Women in North America and the UK*, London and Suffolk: Reality Street Editions.

PERLOFF, Marjorie (1990) 'Canon and loaded gun: feminist poetics and the avant-garde' in *Poetic License: Essays on Modernist and Postmodernist Lyric*, Evanston, IL: Northwestern University Press.

PRESLEY, Frances (1995) *Automatic Cross Stitch* (extracts), Cheltenham: Short Run.

—— (1997) 'What do women want from experimental prose?', paper given at the Sub Voicive Colloquium.

—— (unpublished) 'Grace notes and case notes: the act of noting in the poetry and prose of Elaine Randell'.

RANDELL, Elaine (1987) *Gut Reaction*, Twickenham and Wakefield: North and South.

RETALLACK, Joan (1994) ':RE: THINKING:LITERARY:FEMINISM: (three essays onto shaky grounds)' in **Lynn Keller** and **Cristanne Miller** (1994) editors, *Feminist Measures*, Ann Arbor: University of Michigan Press, pp. 344–77.

RILEY, Denise (1993) *Mop Mop Georgette: New and Selected Poems 1986–1993*, Cambridge and London: Reality Street Editions.

WALDROP, Rosmarie (1993) *Lawn of Excluded Middle*, Providence: Tender Buttons.

WALSH, Catherine (1994) *Pitch*, Durham: Pig Press.

WILLS, Clair (1994) 'Contemporary women's poetry: experimentalism and the expressive voice', *Critical Quarterly*, Vol. 36 No. 3 (Autumn), pp. 34–52.

WOOLF, Virginia (1929) *A Room of One's Own*, Hogarth Press.

Ballad of the Wedding in Marseilles

Michèle Roberts

FEMINIST REVIEW NO 62, SUMMER 1999, ISSN 0141-7789, PP. 113–117

i

There'll be a wedding in Marseilles.
We insist on coming, to witness it:
we three sisters, tall
on a trip without husbands
back in that bedroom bond of
squabbles, a common
speech, able to
screech, mutter, gabble
again in turn, try on
each other's lives
like lipsticks and dresses.

For our relatives we're *les Anglaises*
foreign, funny in
black minis, needing tea.

Past the *zone industrielle's*
cement apartment blocks, the
olive canning factories, to
the *metro's* end: Sainte
Octavie, a village
with plane trees and *place*
swallowed by suburbs.

We've arrived bearing English gifts:
it's *chic* to like whisky.
Here you are, Bertrand, the little
girls' blue-eyed aquiline hero
notre cher oncle, sweet patriarch
shrunken by debt and worry.
Here you are, Marie-Angèle, sharp

redhead bride, *notre chère tante*
worn mother of seven grown children.

Here you are, quiver of virgin aunts
still so pretty at fifty.
(Your losses were early ones:
no lovers to scar you.
'One thing about the Germans –
ils étaient si propres!')
Here you are, babies, who
keep on coming.

Here is the ark
that cannot save me:
le foyer catholique
with its healthy devotion
to folklore and communal meals
its polished *armoires* of prayers
for *drogués* and *prostitutuées*
its phonecalls from houseless
Algerians (these live
in the bad part of town: we must not go there)
its charitable advice
to all those about to drown.

ii

Our little cousin's brow
is bound with silk flowers.
Her gloves are clean
satin, her
anxious acned skin
repressed by pink makeup.
Her wide child's eyes
open on power: this
is birthday, this is becoming.

She marries *le microphone*.
To its black muzzle
she makes her vows:
'*j' ai choisi mon homme*:
I invite him to choose me.'

The cine cameras purr
to guitars, jolly pop-songs.

My ex-favourite cousin says Mass
le bon Dieu to Noah:
'You have dominion
over toute la terre.
Go forth and procreate, and multiply.'
Their union will reproduce itself on video.
The buzz-word is *communauté.*

Now we're praying for souls *en crise*
pour les couples en difficulté but not
for all those who've jumped ship
from the wreck of a marriage
nevertheless I'm baptized by
this Flood, licked at
by mother-tongues, lifted
up, pulled by the hand off
to the *salle paroissiale*, its
bustle of toasts, *saucisson*
and *vin blanc cassis.*

iii

The *mistral* frets down the street.
We drive north for
the feast, the dancing.
Rain blears red earth
and rocks, sweeps the umbrella
pines' vivid green cups.
Brown stylized pics
on the *autoroute*
tell us what we pass by, must miss:
ceci est un vineyard; *ceci*
est un cherry-tree; a symbol
denotes a mystery.

So they sail off in the French family
arche, the new
Monsieur et Madame Noé
after a slide-show
on the young people's holy
mission to *triste* (communist) *Pologne*
in a rainbow of wines
and cake, the fish
dead under pastry *couettes*

the pigs arranged on *nouvelle*
cuisine pillows, the
peas and beans
stuck in *bouquets printanières.*

And certainly there are
no heretics on board
no monsters or artists.
I jive with my *jumelle*
throw her, both laughing
into disciplined spins
and uncertainly we sleep
in the convent dorm's little
mirrorless boxes, a
formica reformatory.

On the plane home I swap
bits of food for gossip: 'Kathleen
the ex-nun
swears you're damned, and
says you'll roast in hell.
Also, gays disgust her.'

But one of my cousins, bow-tied
Emile, the tall beautiful boy
who lives in sin
has given me my French soul.
I carry it carefully through Customs
knobbly as sugared almonds
smelling of *pastis* and
confit de foie de canard
tasting of rain, and juniper
steep as Mont Ventoux, wide
and deep as the Durance
green as the new crop
of *olives cassées.*

© Michèle Roberts
(written in 1987: revised 1997)

Note

Michèle Roberts is a poet, novelist and short-story writer. Her poetry collections
are *The Mirror of the Mother* (Methuen, 1986), *Psyche and the Hurricane*

(Methuen, 1991) and *All the Selves I Was: New and Selected Poems* (Virago, 1995). Her fiction includes *A Piece of the Night* (Women's Press, 1978), *In the Red Kitchen* (1990), *Daughters of the House* (1992; shortlisted for the Booker Prize; winner of the W.H. Smith Literary Award) and *Impossible Saints* (1997).

'Every poem breaks a silence that had to be overcome'*:

The Therapeutic Power of Poetry Writing

Gillie Bolton

FEMINIST REVIEW NO 62, SUMMER 1999, ISSN 0141-7789, PP. 118–133

Abstract

The creation of poetry can be an intensely healing process, as therapeutic as the other arts and talking therapies. This paper examines three areas. First, it sets out some opinions about the specific qualities of poetry that make it particularly valuable as part of a therapeutic process. It goes on to give exemplified information about how poetry is used within healthcare in Britain. Finally, it indicates the current growth of interest in this area, with brief descriptions of pilot research studies where poetry has been offered by a writing therapist, or by nursing or medical practitioners.

Keywords

poetry; therapy; medicine; nursing; research; professional development

The blood jet is poetry.

Sylvia Plath, 1965

Take that old, material utensil, language, found all about you, blank with familiarity, smeared with daily use, and make it into something that means more than it says. What poetry is made of is so old, so familiar, that it's easy to forget that it's not just the words, but polyrhythmic sounds, speech in its first endeavours (every poem breaks a silence that had to be overcome), prismatic meanings lit by each other's light, stained by each other's shadows.

Adrienne Rich, 1995

Poems 'profoundly alter the man or woman who wrote them'.

Dannie Abse, 1998

The writing of poetry profoundly alters the writer because the process faces one with oneself. Poetry is an exploration of the deepest and most intimate experiences, thoughts, feelings, ideas: distilled, pared to succinctness, and made music to the ear by lyricism. Dannie Abse is poet, poetry tutor, and medical practitioner: a combination with powerful precedence (Hudson

Jones, 1997). Poetry and medicine have gone hand in hand since Apollo was the god of both. Now is a time when women are taking and moulding 'that old material, language' in a way which gives us a voice. Adrienne Rich said:

> For women writers in particular, there is the challenge and promise of a whole new psychic geography to be explored. But there is also a difficult and dangerous walking on the ice, as we try to find language and images for a consciousness we are just coming into, and with little in the past to support us.
>
> (Rich, 1980)

This paper explores ways in which this has been taking place therapeutically, and offers a range of examples of women's struggles and writing.

The therapeutic and developmental power of creative writing has been the subject of my research as an academic research fellow in Medical Humanities, over the last ten years. There are two foci to this research: therapeutic writing for patients, and reflective writing for health practitioners (doctors, nurses, therapists, etc.) for professional development. Arts therapies (art, drama, music) have been available in Britain for some time (Payne, 1993; Kaye and Blee, 1997). But writing is only just making a start. Recent research suggests that writing can be as effective as the other arts therapies and psychotherapy (Bolton, 1998a, b, c). The reflective work with health practitioners harnesses the same power of creative writing as in therapeutic writing. Through writing stories and poems about their work, these professionals discover areas about which they need to think and reflect more deeply, on their own through further writing, and in discussion with others in carefully facilitated groups. This enables them to develop their practice, as well as understand themselves and their work more effectively (see Bolton, 1994a, b; Illman, 1996).

This paper examines and illustrates some aspects of my therapeutic writing research which relate to poetry. It also offers some of the theoretical background, and some examples of practice.

Writing poetry is different

The process of writing required of the poet takes the writer into hitherto unexpressed and unexplored areas of experience, in a way only very skilled psychotherapy/analysis or the other arts therapies can. The writing of poetry can also effectively be used to examine issues the writer knows are problematic but does not want to talk about.

There is a range of reasons why poetry has expressive and personally explorative power. The initial stages of poetry writing are often intuitive,

FEMINIST REVIEW NO 62, SUMMER 1999

and unreasoned: this has been likened to dropping a bucket into the well of oneself, pulling it up dripping to see what is there (Sansom, 1994; Byron, 1995). In the evaluation of my Therapeutic Writing in Primary Care Project (more below; Bolton, 1998a), one of the GPs commented: 'the value of the kind of writing this project encourages is that *expression is catharsis*'. It can be safer to do this in writing than in speech. Talking to a piece of paper is much more private: it can't answer back, interrupt, embarrass, or worst of all – remember.

One disadvantage of writing is that the first and perhaps most judgemental audience is the internal critic. Women seem to have a particularly bossy internal schoolteacher ready with a red pen. Virginia Woolf said she had to kill her 'angel in the house' (1942), before she could write effectively. This inner critic told her she should be using her energies caring for others – not self-indulgently scribbling. Everyone has to find their own way of killing their angel, or sacking their schoolteacher.

Poetry can be intended for its writer alone, until she chooses for it to be read by another. As much time as is needed can be taken for private re-reading. It can then be shared with a carefully chosen other: friend, counsellor, or doctor; or it can even be torn up, flushed down the lavatory or burnt without even having been read by its writer.

The therapeutic value of poetry writing is far more than just the catharsis of the initial outpouring of writing. Reworking can bring insight and consolidation. The redrafting of poetry is a powerful, deeply thoughtful process of attempting to capture the experience, emotion, or memory as accurately as possible, in apt poetic words and images. Writing can be worked on in a way neither speech nor thought can, because it leaves footprints on the page, it stays there in the same state as when it was written. Poetry writing can assist clarity of thought and understanding, and offer discipline and a measure of control which can be stabilizing (Lester and Terry, 1992). An issue clarified into words, graphically visualized, and controlled by poetic form is an issue on the way to being dealt with.

Poetry on the page can relate back to its writer (as well as to other readers) more intensely than prose. 'One reacts, not just to what is written but to what seems to hover around it unwritten' (Frampton, 1986) on those suggestive white spaces which accompany a poem on the page.

The very creative process can be exciting and enjoyable; it can increase self-confidence and self-respect. Writing is physical, creating a concrete object; the movement of the pen/cil over the page, and the contemplation of the product, can give pleasure and satisfaction. These factors can energize the writer to deepen still further their explorations and expressions.

And writing does not rush; it is more contemplative than talking. As well as being a satisfying physical creative process, the writing hand not only seems to know what the thinking mind does not, but also knows how much that mind, as well as the feeling heart, can bear to face. We in the West, since the Enlightenment, have tended to rely on our cognitive powers, as well as to believe we can understand and manipulate our world and ourselves (body *and* mind). Western medical and psychiatric understanding has not been holistic, and patients have not been expected to be involved as primary actors in their own diagnosis and treatment. Therapeutic writing asks the writer to trust their body, through their writing hand, not only to tell them vital things about themselves, but also to offer routes to connecting up and making whole. Therapeutic writing is an act of faith in the self. In the ten years I have been working in therapeutic writing I have never known anyone write anything which is not the right thing – painful and distressing to deal with perhaps – but always right for that writer at that time. Poetry can create order out of mental turmoil or strife; poets have explained this as a reason for choosing such tight poetic forms as sonnet, vilanelle or haiku.

Poetry can be a focus for intense and fruitful discussion with the right reader or group. This reader must be chosen with care; a relative or lover may well be the wrong choice (Bolton, 1998a).

Therapy or art?

Not all therapeutic writing is art, just as not all poetry is therapeutic. The cathartic splurge of any writer is not necessarily a poem, even if it doesn't reach the right-hand margin of the page. The crafting stages of writing – redrafting and editing – are generally essential to develop the raw personal notes into material which looks outwards and can communicate with a reader. A bleeding heart poured out on a page is likely to be therapeutic, but may well not be a poem. Personal angst will probably have to be written out of any poem before it can communicate publicly: the reader is not interested in the writer herself, but in what she has to say.

Many beginning poets dream of getting published; they need to be supported through this stage to an acceptance that the first stages of writing is primarily for themselves. Generally only an experienced poet has the knowledge and skill to write for an audience from first draft. Tentative and personally explorative first drafts are usually likely to create the most effective poems. If beginning poets concentrate only on getting published they will probably never experience the therapeutic value, nor write anything worth publishing.

FEMINIST REVIEW NO 62, SUMMER 1999

Many poets expostulate that writing is an art, not a therapy: a process only undertaken for artistic purposes. I do not believe poetry needs protecting in this way. Much poetry has a very clear therapeutic base, exploring issues which are also vital to the reader; Jackie Kay, for example, addresses her own experience of adoption and blackness (1991). Few poets will tell you they habitually write to publish. They will say they write because they have to: the words come compulsively and have to be written and rewritten until what is hovering in the mind is on the page as clearly as possible. *It's better out than in* is a saying often heard; there are ducts other than tears. The fact that the act of writing can be therapeutic to the writer at certain stages does not denigrate the art; conversely it adds passion and intensity to the writing.

Anne Sexton was encouraged to write poetry by her psychiatrist, whom she remembered saying: 'You can't kill yourself, you have something to give. Why if people read your poems (they were all about how sick I was) they would think, "there's somebody else like me!" They wouldn't feel alone.' Her biographer continues: 'This was the message Sexton called her turning point: "I had found something to *do* with my life" ' (Middlebrook, 1992). She revised her poems extensively – typically twenty or more drafts; the *form* of poetry was vital to her: 'As she perfected her poems she was, perhaps, able to achieve an intellectual distancing from and control over the emotions that initially stimulated the content of the poems' (Lester and Terry, 1992).

Sexton has been labelled a 'confessional poet' who described tabooed aspects of life too intimately. Yet she said: 'I, who reportedly write so truthfully about myself, so openly, am not that open' (Middlebrook, 1992). Anne Sexton's poems were not confessional outpourings leaking upon the prissy world without her cognisance. The initial writings may well have been, and probably were, raw cries of pain, anger, distress, joy: possibly 'confessions', but not *poetry*. Her published poems were artefacts – carefully created to achieve the effect they did. This, it has been argued, helped to keep her from suicide until she was 46.

Timings and stages

There is a time for writing poetry. I often ask people who are occasional poets what kind of life event or emotion encourages (or forces them) to write. It is nearly always one of the extremes – despair or unhappiness – a stillbirth, or falling in love.

The stage at which it is appropriate to write about these vital life issues is also important. When life goes disastrously wrong, or wonderfully right, the emotions tend to be intense, experience of events jumbled: writing at this time may be cathartically useful – but it may not be possible to craft a poem. Written notes taken at this time will be extremely useful later. There is, conversely, a time when it is too late to write. Events and their attendant emotions and experiences become indistinct, lose their force; if they are too *hot* to handle as poetry earlier, they can equally become too *cool* later. There is a right time in between: Wordsworth referred to this when he spoke of 'emotion recollected in tranquillity' (1976: 22).

Poetry is particularly appropriate at certain milestones such as adolescence (Fuchel, 1985; Atlas *et al.*, 1992), birth (see below), and near death (Sluder, 1990; Frampton, 1986; and see below).

The stages of writing poetry – when to write first draft notes, when to craft a poem, when to redraft critically and analytically, when to take the advice of trusted others – all have their appropriate timing. Timing, an essential element of the poetry writing process, cannot be forced. It is as though the writing hand has a direct connection with the belly or heart, missing out that critical brain: 'The still dumb flow of writing passes through my woman's body, searching for words' (Cixous, 1989).

Poetry writing is particularly appropriate for the depressed, the anxious, or those suffering from certain illnesses, physical or psychological. *Survivors Poetry* is an organization for survivors of mental distress, and it is also run by those survivors. They have recently collaborated in a collection of poetry edited by Ken Smith and Matthew Sweeney (1997) mainly drawing on work created by the patients or users of the Bethlem and Maudsley hospitals. The introduction notes that: 'Creative work produced in this way is rarely considered in its own right and tends to be dismissed as "merely therapy", an example of the stigma which surrounds mental illness.' Felix Post in his Foreword refers to his own research which indicates that writers have far more psychiatric problems and illnesses than the rest of the population, but that poets suffered least of all writers (Post, 1996). This, he suggests, might be the psychotherapeutic effect of: 'putting into harmonious and rhythmical language one's own inner sufferings and distress in the concentrated form of the lyric poem' (Smith and Sweeney, 1997). The poet-editors of the anthology refer to research which says that 'poets are thirty times more likely to undergo a depressive illness than the rest of the population'. It is beyond the scope of this paper to address whether this means that poetry drives us insane, or that a very large number of mentally ill people turn to poetry writing; but I would incline towards the latter. This is an under-researched area which deserves more scrutiny.

Writing on prescription

A pilot research project training general practitioners (GPs) has been undertaken to offer therapeutic writing to depressed and anxious patients (Bolton, 1998a, b; Fursland, 1996; Illman, 1996). By writing, patients could take some control over their own treatment, in their own time and at their own pace. The doctors found it to be a cheap, straightforward, effective and not time-consuming intervention, once they were used to understanding how, when and to which patients to suggest it. The patient had to be willing and able to take some control over their own symptoms and treatment; and the writing had to be offered in a non-prescriptive, open, inviting way, with time for reflection. The GPs felt the timing of the suggestion had to be sensitively handled, or the patient might experience the doctor as giving them 'homework'. The GPs found it most useful to patients who were suffering from problematic life circumstances rather than chronic settled depression. We found it was not appropriate for very disturbed or psychotic patients: they needed more supervision than a GP could offer. I was not privy to the patients' writing on the whole, though one patient has permitted his work and attitude to it to be published (Bolton, 1998a); another paper is in preparation, written jointly by a patient, their GP, and myself.

A couple of workshops in a GP surgery for *New Mums* was part of this project. Six or eight mothers, their babies, and some toddlers attended the hour long workshop, along with the GP, the practice nurse and the health visitor (all women). One of the mothers wrote a graphic poem about her father dying very close to the birth of her baby. It was read to the group, and received with a great deal of feeling and support; my later feedback from the GP was that the mother had found it extremely helpful. Two of the mothers later published their writings: one about her child having meningitis (Dudley, 1997), and the other about having a Down's Syndrome baby (Brunt, 1998). The latter (written after the session, as I encouraged the group to continue writing) describes the heartaches and joys of parenting such a baby. It is not a poem, but there are certainly poetic passages in it: 'I didn't want people to say *I'm sorry*. If you met Lucy, you'd know why there's no need to be sorry.'

Therapeutic writing for the dying

Another pilot project researching the power of therapeutic writing was in *palliative care*: carried out in a hospice. Creative writing, particularly poetry, is particularly appropriate for people at the ends of their lives when the need to express, clarify, and understand is very strong. It helps them to reflect back, recollect and reintegrate their present self with their past selves, to reminisce constructively, and gain a sense of wholeness and fullness of life. Its succinctness and lyricism make it particularly appropriate (Birren and Deutchmann, 1991; Sluder, 1990).

Many patients grasped and were able to make use of writing to tackle a range of problems. I found these varied from family issues (e.g. making peace with relatives to whom pain has been given in the past), to issues relating to the disease (e.g. coming to terms with having cancer), to pain control, and the distress, anxiety, and depression caused by the disease (Bolton, 1998b, c; Boxsall, 1997). Below is the experience of a patient who used poetry to explore her troubled, yet at times intensely joyous, inner self.

Jan Broadwood was a day patient (later in-patient), who had had, and was having, a tough life. Jan was open, flexible, and keen to develop her use of writing. She had belonged to writers' groups and was used to a didactic approach from her tutors. We worked together both in small groups in the day-centre, and one-to-one. At one of the first groups I offered a suggestion for writing, after some discussion. Jan responded quickly: 'that's a bit open, I need you to be more precise'. I answered: 'just put your pen on the paper and see what comes'. She did; we never looked back.

Jan trusted me to have a stab at writing without a structure. She had not tried personal and explorative writing before, and much of what she wrote was dark and involved: full of blood-red, spiders, being shut up in boxes. She always wanted a *homework* theme to take away with her; I once suggested 'a happy memory', because her writing was habitually so dark. She was initially unable to write anything, but eventually redrafted her piece to this:

One memory too short

From prison I'm free, free, free.
Through the orchard of stunted trees.
Staggering out into the field,
there suddenly appeared a tiny hill.

Scrabbled to the top as best I was able,
standing straight with arms outstretched.
The sweet smell of earth bourne on the breeze hit me,

then I reeled.

Sheer pleasure – but it didn't last long –

I fell to my knees and knew polio had won.

FEMINIST REVIEW NO 62, SUMMER 1999

with curling finger the hospital beckons,
the memory of happiness will live forever.

Jan Broadwood

A volunteer, who was very close to Jan and had been involved in our discussions from the start, hoped she might cut the reference to the polio, but Jan knew what she wanted – the transition from joy to sad knowledge. Jan commented: 'I tried to write you something happy, Gillie, and look what happened.'

The next poem Jan wrote was in the voice of a homeless girl living in a cardboard box, confined to a tiny space; it expresses her frustration with her own life, particularly these lines:

No Escape

Every day the ceiling gets lower, lower
   'till I could scream with the power
      it possesses over me.
Please tell me what am I going to do?
   just smile and say 'I'm fine –
     'how are you?'

Jan Broadwood

Writing as a reflective health professional

Reflection upon practice is seen as an essential element to the development of practice in medicine and nursing. Marrying creative writing with reflective practice in the courses I run for doctors, nurses and other professionals creates a dynamic and vivid professional development process. Group members write expressive and explorative pieces (poetry or story) about their work, and then read and discuss them with each other in a carefully facilitated group. The groups are always closed and small; they are either run as in-service training (Brimacombe, 1996; Purdy, 1996; Heller, 1997) or as part of Medical Masters programmes (Bolton, 1994a; Fox, 1993).

A group of women health professionals

Two women who had experienced my reflective writing courses asked me to run a weekend for them, and their women's group – as people, as women – with less professional focus. I therefore focused it on writing for personal and spiritual development, midway between therapeutic and the reflective practice writing, more similar to an annual course I run for The Society of Friends (Bolton and Padfield, 1996). The difference is almost entirely in the area I ask people to write about; with a professional group I also emphasize that this is *not* a therapeutic group.

As a writing *starter* this group wrote about the different hats they wear in their lives, the different people they are in different settings and groupings: mother, health visitor, lover, daughter . . . , and the people they might have been. I always ask people to write without thinking, to allow their hand to take over: thinking inhibits this kind of writing. We then have plenty of time to reread silently and privately before deciding what to read to the rest of the group. The writings are then discussed: focusing on the writing rather than the person. This creates a safe space for the writer, who knows they will not be questioned or discussed beyond the limits of the writing they have chosen to share. And the groups are always bounded by confidentiality.

This particular weekend was intense and dynamic; I was also able to work through important issues for myself in my own writing during the weekend, supported by the group. This is very rare, and a tribute to the group, as I can usually write myself *or* facilitate, but not both.

> We are a close group of friends sharing a background in health. We didn't really know what we were letting ourselves in for. Two of us had worked with Gillie in the past, and trusted her completely. All we knew was that we wanted to learn and be together and explore the connection between writing and our feelings as women and friends rather than as health professionals. The experience took us all on different personal journeys, often intense and painful, but always within the safety net of Gillie's facilitation.
>
> Kate Billingham

Liz Perkins wrote a poem during the Saturday, a poem which was waiting for the right environment to be written and shared. She tells of the process:

> If you'd asked me before the weekend about the issues in this poem, I'd have said they were sleeping peacefully. I'd done a lot of work on them; they pop up from time to time for a bit more, but on the whole – fairly sorted. I'd written poetry before, when my marriage was breaking up, and learnt a lot about the satisfactions that come with getting the feelings on paper and revising till the shape feels right. I'd done nothing much for ages, though writing prose is part (too much perhaps) of my professional academic life, and I'd lately been feeling that it would be good to get back to poems. The first day of the weekend went smoothly for me – I found my feet (or my voice?) again, wrote something subacid and satisfying to me about the process of academic writing, and went to sleep well pleased.
>
> I woke early and distressed, with the memory of a dream I'd had as my marriage shredded. This poem was the result.

The might-have-beens

Buried under the apple tree
The might-have-beens,

Deformed dead babies.
Not for them the blue of childhood comforter
But grey finality for shroud.

Sandie Shaw hair that curled improperly
Buried in my brother's grave.

Volunteer for sun and colour
Buried in my marriage

Breasts leaking milk, throttled back
Buried in the wasteland of divorce.

There are many fruitful apple trees
Death dug in to nourish life.
Sleep sweetly, children;
While I, relinquishing,
Put flowers on your graves
Occasionally.

(Perkins, 1999)

I had been very hesitant to talk about childlessness, having tried on a few occasions when the pain was worse and received staggeringly insensitive responses from apparently trustworthy people. The sense of shame and humiliation is hard to shift, and I've found it's easier on me and on other people not to talk about it. I'd passed up an opportunity on the first day of this weekend, not wanting to bother to package issues for easy sympathy, and not wanting either to set up an investment of time and energy that wasn't on anyone's official agenda for the weekend. By the next morning, no-one had much choice!

It's been a useful poem, for me – and more useful because sharing it was an inevitable part of the process of writing it. I even did as I was told about publishing it, which was certainly the last thing I'd had in mind at the time. 'Every poem breaks a silence that had to be overcome. . .'

Elizabeth Perkins

Image in poetry

Poetry uses image to explicate and convey complex emotional and mental happenings. I have heard the poet-doctor William Carlos Williams said: 'no ideas but in things'. T.S. Eliot called this process the *objective correlative* (1951). An idea, emotion, feeling or thought is not presented in the abstract – but as a concrete, graspable entity. The power of poetry lies partly in this, both to the writer and the reader.

Jan Broadwood used the image of climbing up the tiny hill to represent freedom, and living in a cardboard box for being trapped. The reader has a pair of pictures in her mind – far more powerful than if Jan had merely told us she felt trapped, and had had a glimpse of freedom in the past.

Liz Perkins' 'apple trees' are a poignant image of life in the midst of death – her babies were 'might-have-beens' but those of other women swelled and grew to ripeness, to be set 'going like a fat gold watch' (Plath, 1965).

Jacqueline Brown has written a graphic sequence about childlessness, *Thinking Egg* (1993), using egg images throughout. Here is a chilling image of a woman at her marriage: 'she cannot forsee the moment/when she will be cracked and eaten'.

Sappho must have been one of the earliest writers to use image in writing for therapeutic benefit. A wealth of loneliness is carried by the last three words of this:

> The moon has set
> > and the stars have faded
> midnight has gone,
> > long hours pass by, pass by;
> I sleep alone
>
> (Sappho, trans, 1992)

Writing and health

Many projects have taken place in Britain and Ireland, but unfortunately most reports are not readily available. Some available texts are Kaye and Blee (1997), Hunt and Sampson (1998), and Kline (1996). Funding comes from various sources such as the National Lottery; my own has been supported by The Royal College of General Practitioners, Continuing Medical Education, and Health Trusts. There seem to be more and more institutions interested in funding such initiatives. The Poetry Society (see Fursland, 1997), and some of the regional arts boards (e.g. Yorkshire and Humberside) are funding projects in arts and health. Most poets are very keen to share their time, skills, experience, and knowledge of the way writing can help personal exploration. Many run workshops in educational settings (university, continuing education, WEA), and increasingly in health settings (e.g. hospices, hospitals, mental health institutions and community, old people's homes). Only a minority of poets, however, would say their focus is therapeutic; nearly all would emphasize that they are facilitating and nurturing poetry – the therapeutic aspect is a private spin-off for the writer. This is not only reasonable, it is sensible: they are poets not therapists.

Ethics

The ethics of therapeutic writing facilitation are complex. Poetry gives access to vital issues which can temporarily cause distress and occasionally psychological imbalance. These are usually short term, and an inevitable aspect of the process of dealing with deep-seated psychological problems. Handled professionally and sensitively, this can be a process of personal growth for the writer. The ethical issues of facilitation need to be tackled; Fiona Sampson has touched upon them (Hunt and Sampson, 1998). Ethical guidelines are being set up by LAPIDUS (the Association for the Literary Arts in Personal Development) and other organizations such as St Joseph's Hospice, Hackney; and these will be amongst the issues studied in my next research.

There is no organized 'poetry therapy' in Britain; in the USA the National Association of Poetry Therapy offers an ethical code. Writing therapy is one of the areas being worked on by the 'Humanities in Medicine' Initiative, spearheaded by the Chief Medical Officer of the NHS, a group of forty professionals from health and health-related therapeutic fields. 'Plans to offer "arts on prescription" throughout the UK are being developed', as part of 'a strategy to promote the arts from the margins into the very heart of healthcare planning, policy-making and practice' (Wyn Owen, 1998). There will be a book published by the Nuffield Trust early next year reporting on progress to date, to be followed by a lengthy handbook.

Last words

Research and development continues. The aim is to undertake medical trials, which will bring 'therapeutic writing' to the notice of the medical canon.

> The physician and the poet can both be healers. They share a common goal in their efforts to maintain light and order against the chaos of darkness and disease, and to create or restore the beauty and harmony of health: in this quest, medicine serves the body, poetry the spirit.
>
> (Hudson Jones, 1997)

Anne Hudson Jones (Professor of Medical Humanities) is, I feel, working on the same awareness as Adrienne Rich. In writing poetry we take our holistic spiritual, psychological, and physical well-being into our own hands and hearts: a feminist approach to health, counterposing the prevailing scientific, post-enlightenment attitudes.

Depression is a passive response. Writing poetry is a way of grasping life, nurturing every bit of good, connecting up severed bits of ourselves; it is written from our whole self – mind, spirit and body. Poetry, even when it concerns death, pain disfigurement, despair, is vibrant, alive, a way of life.

Acknowledgements

I would like to thank Jan Broadwood and all the patients and health professionals who were involved in the studies; Liz Perkins for generously contributing; Marilyn Lidster for support; Vicki Bertram, Kate Billingham, David Hart, Blair Smith, Leah Thorn, Chris Woods, for vital editorial help; Stephen Rowland for mental, spiritual and literal food and wine.

Notes

Gillie Bolton is research fellow in Medical Humanities at the Institute of General Practice and Primary Care, Sheffield University. Having read Social Anthropology, she moved from teaching infants, school refusers and gypsies into higher education. Her own writing experience, as well as teaching Creative Writing both at Sheffield Hallam University English Department, and at Northern College (one of the eight Residential Colleges for unemployed people who missed out on education when young) taught her the therapeutic power of focusing on the content of personal writing. She now researches therapeutic writing for patients, and reflective writing for practitioners. She is a member of Sir Kenneth Calman's initiative: 'Humanities in Medicine', ex-chair of the National Association of Writers in Education, and an award winning published poet.

* Quotation in title from Rich (1995).

References

ABSE, D. (1998) 'More than a green placebo' *The Lancet*, Vol. 351, No. 9099, pp. 362–4.
ATLAS, J.A., SMITH, P. and SESSOMS, L. (1992) 'Art and poetry in brief therapy of hospitalised adolescents' *The Arts in Psychotherapy*, Vol. 19, pp. 279–83.
BIRREN, J. and DEUTCHMAN, D. (1991) *Guiding Autobiography Groups for Older Adults*, Maryland: Johns Hopkins University Press.
BOLTON, G. (1998a) 'Writing not pills: writing therapy in primary care' in C. Hunt and F. Samson (1998) editors, *The Self on the Page: Theory and Practice of Creative Writing in Personal Development*. London: Jessica Kingsley, pp. 78–92.
—— (1998b) *The Therapeutic Potential of Creative Writing: Writing Myself*, London: Jessica Kingsley.
—— (1998c) 'I said it in writing: therapeutic writing in the hospice' in T. Greenhalgh and B. Hurwitz *Narrative Based Medicine: Dialogue and Discourse in Clinical Practice*: London: BMJ Publications.
—— (1994a) 'Stories at work: fictional~critical writing as a means of professional development' *British Education Research Journal*, Vol. 20, No. 1, pp. 55–68.
—— (1994b) 'Stories at work: writing fiction for professional development' *Issues in Social Work Education*, Vol. 14, No. 2, pp. 21–33.

BOLTON, G. and PADFIELD, D. (1996) *Reflections in Writing*, Kelso: Curlew Press.

BOXSHALL, J. (1997) 'Lean on me' *Here's Health*, October, pp. 34–7.

BRIMACOMBE, M. (1996) 'The emotional release of writing' *GP*, December.

BROWN, J. (1993) *Thinking Egg*, Todmorden, Lancs: Littlewood Arc, p. 19.

BRUNT, L. (1998) 'The birth of Lucy' *CNCF Magazine*, Summer pp. 5–6.

BYRON, C. (1995) in S. Thomas *Creative Writing: A Handbook for Workshop Leaders*, pp. 1–5.

CIXOUS, H. (1989) 'Writing as a second heart' in S. Sellers (1989) editor, *Delighting the Heart*, London: The Women's Press, p. 198.

DUDLEY, K. (1997) 'Our son had meningitis' *Practical Parenting*, July, pp. 85–88.

ELIOT, T.S. (1951) *Selected Essays*, London: Faber, p. 145.

FOX, N. (1993) *Postmodernism, Sociology and Health*, Buckingham: Open University Press, pp. 114–15.

FRAMPTON, D.R. (1986) 'Restoring creativity to the dying patient' *British Medical Journal*, Vol. 93, pp. 1593–5.

FUCHEL, J.C. (1985) 'Writing poetry can enhance the psychotherapeutic process' *The Arts in Psychotherapy*, Vol. 12, pp. 89–93.

FURSLAND, E. (1996) 'Textual Healing' *Here's Health*, August, pp. 44–6.

—— (1997) 'An ode to healing' *Guardian*, 14 October.

HELLER, T. (1997) 'The arts as reflective practice' *Serious Fun: The Arts in Primary Health Care*, Yorkshire and Humberside Arts, pp. 28–9.

HUDSON JONES, A. (1997) 'Literature and medicine: physician-poets' *The Lancet*, Vol. 349, pp. 275–8.

HUNT, C. and SAMPSON, F. (1998) editors, *The Self on the Page: Theory and Practice of Creative Writing in Personal Development*, London: Jessica Kingsley.

ILLMAN, J. (1996) 'The doctor's gentle inscription' *Guardian*, 19 March, p. 10.

KAY, J. (1991) *The Adoption Papers*, Newcastle Upon Tyne: Bloodaxe.

KAYE, C. and BLEE, T. (1997) *The Arts in Health Care*, London: Jessica Kingsley.

KLINE, H. (1996) 'Mistakes and successes: writing with adults with learning disabilities' *Writing in Education*, Vol.9, pp. 28–31.

LESTER, D. and TERRY, R. (1992) 'The use of poetry therapy: lessons from the life of Anne Sexton' *The Arts in Psychotherapy*, Vol.19, pp. 47–52.

MIDDLEBROOK, D.W. (1992) *Anne Sexton: A Biography*, London: Virago pp. 42–3.

PAYNE, H. (1993) *Handbook of Inquiry in the Arts Therapies: One River Many Currents*, London: Jessica Kingsley.

PERKINS, L. (1999) 'The might-have-beens' *Progress in Palliative Care*, Vol. 7, No. 1, p. 40.

PLATH, S. (1965) *Ariel* (Morning Song), London: Faber & Faber, p. 11.

—— (1981) *Collected Poems* (Kindness), London: Faber & Faber, pp. 269-70.

POST, F. (1996) 'Verbal creativity, depression and alcoholism: an investigation of one hundred American and British writers' *British Journal of Psychiatry*, Vol.168, pp. 545–55.

PURDY, R. (1996) 'Writing refreshes my practice' *Medical Monitor*, March.

RICH, A. (1980) *On Lies, Secrets and Silence: Selected Prose 1966–1978*, London: Virago. p. 35.

—— (1995) *What is Found There: Notebooks on Poetry and Politics*. London: Virago, p. 84.

SANSOM, P. (1994) *Writing Poems*, Newcastle on Tyne: Bloodaxe.

SAPPHO (1992) *Poems and Fragments* edited by J. Balmer, Newcastle on Tyne: Bloodaxe Books, p. 48.

SLUDER, H. (1990) 'The write way: using poetry for self-disclosure' *Journal of Psychosocial Nursing*, Vol. 28, No. 7, pp. 26–8.

SMITH, K. and SWEENEY, M. (1997) editors, *Beyond Bedlam*, London: Anvil, pp. 13–18.

WOOLF, V. (1992[1942]) *The Crowded Dance of Modern Life*, London: Penguin.

WORDSWORTH, W. (1976) *The Lyrical Ballads* (preface), edited by D. Roper, Plymouth: Macdonald & Evans, p. 22, lines 26–7.

WYN OWEN, J. (1998) *The Role of Humanities in Medicine* (leaflet), London: Nuffield Trust.

Reviews

FEMINIST REVIEW NO 62, SUMMER 1999, ISSN 0141-7789, PP. 134–141

How German is She? Post-War West German Reconstruction and the Consuming Woman

Erica Carter
University of Michigan Press: Ann Arbor, March 1998
ISBN 0 472 10755 0 £42.50 (Hbk)

Published in the series 'Social History, Popular Culture, and Politics in Germany', Erica Carter's book is a much needed contribution to the field of German popular culture where there are hardly any publications in English language. Introducing the methodologies of British cultural studies, her study is also a very welcome addition to established critical practice which in German is still dominated by Frankfurt School Marxism and political economy. In an interdisciplinary approach which combines the politico-economic with an analysis of discursive strategies of deviance and resistance, Carter's 'cultural history of femininity in the post-war consumer economy' (xii) examines the unacknowledged active role played by women in the reconstruction of (West) Germany between 1945 and 1960.

Her argument revolves around the contention that the construction of post-war West German national identity centred on the reconstruction of the Federal Republic as a social market economy (in contrast to the socialist GDR) where participation in free market processes was formulated in official discourses of economic policy as an important basis for citizen status. Since women's primary economic function was perceived as consumers in the family, Carter argues that a definition of the citizen as consumer endorsed a sexual division of citizenship which was upheld by social and legal agencies in employment and constitutional law. Despite the exclusion of women from public forms of power, Carter rejects the common interpretation of women's enforced domestication as victimization and insists on a reassessment of the value of housewives' labour and domestic consumption, in particular that their restricted citizenship as domestic consumers also established them as model citizens whose contribution to economic and cultural regeneration was both crucial and public.

How German Is She? is divided into two parts, and in part I Carter identifies the normative processes of identity formation in public representations of the housewife as a rational consumer whose informed choice of products of both quality and low cost contributed decisively to macroeconomic health by regulating free market forces. Part II pits against the official discourses of constitutional law, parliamentary debate, economic policy and market research of part I a series of critical readings of the role of the consuming housewife where consumption is shown as both regulatory practice and identificatory transgressive pleasure. In a wide range of texts which cover urban design, shopping, advertising, fashion, photography, newspaper articles, autobiographical accounts, jazz and melodrama, Carter shows, in narrowly argued and extensively cross-referenced analyses, how the rational consumer housewife was consistently opposed to the irrationally consuming woman whose excess threatened the process of nation building.

In all of these, woman functions as a compromise formation, containing both aspects of apparently irreconcilable opposites; she is thus both signifier for the nation as well as its threatening other and is marked by ambiguity. Carter argues that West Germany constructed its identity primarily against the 'other' of the socialist East (Germany) and the divided city of Berlin was one of the prime sites for symbolic boundary marking. Reading the city as cultural space and political identity, Carter contrasts the tightly planned classically based design of the monumental spaces of central East Berlin with the deliberately un-planned modern design of West Berlin as de-centred suburban sites of consumption which provided universal equal access to prosperity and symbolized the social market principle of consumer democracy. Misuse of these symbolic sites, in the form of shoplifting or irresponsible buying, thus constituted a transgression of the economic order and a threat to the symbolic space of the nation. Since sites of consumption were inhabited primarily by female shoppers, all women were seen to contain the seeds of disorder but especially refugee women from the East whose transgressions in the economic realm were consistently linked with political crime.

Further examples of such deviant femininity as a threat to national identity are traced by Carter in melodrama and fashion where the frugal housewife is cast in binary opposition to the sensual luxury consumer, the lady of *haute couture* fashion or the (working-class) teenage consumer of mass fashion whose various forms of otherness was confirmed by difference articulated through ethnicity, class and age. Inevitably, ranging across such

FEMINIST REVIEW NO 62, SUMMER 1999

a wide array of texts does not allow as detailed an analysis as one would wish. Nevertheless, Carter's development of her argument across such a wide range of discursive sites is impressive and convincing, particularly as she establishes a web-like cross-substantiation with the figure of the rational consumer as its symbolic centre and other. However, such a structure also lays itself open to the danger of self-referentiality, especially as there is a suggestion of a perhaps limited range of source materials. In particular, I would have appreciated an indication of a larger body of texts from which examples were chosen in the analysis of melodrama to support the very interesting points made. It is also in this section that there is a sense of haste – illustrations do not concur with textual description or are wrongly captioned.

But as Carter points out in her conclusion, her study is a 'beginning, . . . a mapping of the terrain of possible future inquiry' (242). *How German Is She?* is an invaluable introduction which students of German popular culture and politics will appreciate. Meticulously flagging up the argument and a constant summarizing of points made means that chapters can be read on their own and the bibliography is wide ranging and very useful.

Karen Seago

Sacrificial Logics, Feminist Theory and the Critique of Identity

Allison Weir

Routledge: London and New York, February 1996
ISBN 0 415 90862 0 £37.50 (Hbk) ISBN 0 415 90863 9 £11.99 (Pbk)

Tracing through and getting underneath the various arguments and implicit assumptions that have formed many feminist theoretical frameworks is one of the strengths of Allison Weir's *Sacrificial Logics*. Two main preoccupations structure Weir's argument: first, a continual questioning of the assumptions which lead to the suppositions that identity and specifically female identity is only ever formed by repression, denial and submission to the patriarchal order, in other words, that female identity is only ever sacrificial. Second, a pressing concern with how women can become more active and engage in social relations which would change the world more effectively. These two preoccupations, as conceptualized by Weir, are neither distant nor incompatible from each other. For her, the continual stress on sacrifice, repression, denial of the female voice and women's incapacity to act and be in the social sphere has led to a theoretical and political impasse in which possibilities and political opportunities cannot be

realized.

Allison Weir takes on boldly and carefully a particular strand within feminist theory as represented by Butler, Kristeva, Benjamin, Chodorow and Irigaray. Weir uses a philosophical lens to explore issues of separation, autonomy, inter-relatedness and connection in order to describe the historical development of, and to question the assumptions embedded in, much contemporary work on female identity. Her confrontation focuses on questioning the contemporary emphasis upon and fetishization of difference and separation. Indeed, she asks, why do we continually assume that the development of a sense of self requires the repression of connection to others? Weir is critical of Benjamin and Chodorow's tendency to run together separation with a severance of connection. For Weir there need not be a difference between being distinct from, and connected to, others and she argues that what is missed from many frameworks is the recognition that the other is a subject like myself: that we are all subjects and objects. Despite their apparent differences, feminists rely on intersubjective theory and those dependent on deconstruction share certain assumptions. Weir argues that

> (T)hese two positions are commonly considered to be diametrically opposed: relational feminists uphold a humanist ideal of intersubjective connection and wholeness, deconstructivists reject such ideals as manifestations of an identitarian logic which represses fragmentation, multiplicity, and difference. Both, however, share in common the view that self-identity is based, necessarily, on a repression or negation of the other. (24)

It is Weir's concern with this negation of the other that motivates her to question the attachment to this theoretical stance. She is concerned that so much theoretical work is based on identity as negation and exclusion and asks pertinently whether Butler and Irigaray are right to argue that to take up any position on identity is necessarily repressive of non-identity and difference? Weir argues that Butler's reliance on Derrida's argument that it is impossible to conceptualize identity means that she cannot conceive a relationship between identity and difference, identity and non-identity which is non-repressive and non-dominating. For Weir it is important that as women we speak with assurance and she is, therefore, dismissive of Irigaray's refusal to struggle for intelligibility. Weir argues that it is important that we take responsibility for our utterances and the meanings that we produce and, further, that this is not necessarily to submit to the patriarchal order. These concerns lead her to a sympathetic reading of Kristeva, who, for Weir, argues that recognition and acceptance are essential to any true relationship, separation can only be a product of a recognition and acceptance of the otherness of the other. The paradox is that we can only become separate by recognizing our connections and joined with others by knowing our distinctiveness. Weir calls for a different conceptualization of

FEMINIST REVIEW NO 62, SUMMER 1999

femininity which takes into account the paradoxical nature of female sub-
jectivity, women's emotional and social experiences and capacities.

Weir's systematic trawl through complex feminist theory confronts many
basic assumptions upon which many of us rely. The book, however, is
repetitive. A second weakness concerns the book's reliance on cognition
and conscious knowledge means that it bypasses difficult theoretical ques-
tions on identity, unconscious identifications, aspects of our being such as
absence and lack, and how these unconscious processes structure, along-
side the social, how we recognize self and other, speak, act, feel and
become. I would have liked a longer section of the book to be spent
analysing and thinking through the challenges that Weir sets us: what
would a theory that would take adequate account of difference and simi-
larity, various experiences and social positioning look like in detail? Weir's
arguments are embedded in and spoken through others and it is ironic,
given her own project, that she so argues for her own position in opposi-
tion to others. Weir, however, rightly stresses the importance of responsi-
bility, commitment, relationship between self and other: intersubjectivity
itself. There continue to be important issues for contemporary feminism in
terms of mapping out a more complex field which takes fuller account of
the multiplicity of identities and experiences in order for political and
social action to be realized effectively and Weir raises a number of impor-
tant issues to help the process.

Amal Treacher

The Threshold of the Visible World

Kaja Silverman

Routledge: London and New York, March 1996
ISBN 0 415 910382 (Hbk) 0 415 910390 (Pbk)

The Threshold of the Visible World by Kaja Silverman is an ambitious
work. Ambitious in her analysis of how we are all positioned in the social
order through visual representation – photography, film and video – and
also ambitious in staking an ethical demand. The theoretical references are
wide-ranging, including those theorists we would expect, Freud and Lacan,
Laura Mulvey and Benjamin. It is refreshing, however, to find the concepts
of Paul Schilder, Wallon and Winnicott together with examples of the film-
makers Ulrike Ottinger, Isaac Julian, Chris Marker and Harun Farocki. It
is a strength of the text that it is ethically motivated and directed towards
inspiring political action.

Silverman's premise is that we need a more radical ethics founded on identification with those whom the social order decrees as unacceptable, whilst also recognizing each individual's distinct autonomy. *If I say 'I am like you', how can we ever be sure that we do not do violence?* This cannot be accomplished by will and determination alone because the act of such an identification challenges us all too deeply. The ethical demand involves the very structure of the self and body-image. Silverman therefore turns to psychoanalysis and theories of representation.

Identification with another according to Freud is brought about through a process of introjection, that is the other is metaphorically consumed or 'eaten up'. *Heteropathic identification* is the opposite, the subject gives away her/himself to another in a state of fascination. Silverman presents an alternative *'identification at a distance'* which preserves both 'subject' and 'object' as separate people. This forms the keystone of Silverman's ethical argument.

Who we identify with is governed by the system of ideals. According to Freud, the ego is the residue of identifications, thus the bodily ego is itself formed in relation to cultural norms and ideals. Silverman refers to the work of two neglected analysts, Paul Schilder and Henri Wallon. Schilder's *The Image and Appearance of the Human Body*, is a most extraordinary work of 1935 which discusses the experience of body-image and its relation to physical sensation. It is this ownership of physical experience which Wallon terms the *proprioceptive* ego. Unlike much contemporary theory in which the subject may apparently exist in perpetual transformation of, for example her/his sexual position or gender, Silverman points out the fundamental experience of *one's own body*. This unfashionable viewpoint suggests that our capacity to identify with another is limited by fear of losing our bodily integrity.

The experience of the body-image is governed by *ideals*; body norms based on ideals of beauty, health and wholeness. Giving a personal example Silverman describes her walk to college through the homeless of Telegraph Avenue. The dilemma of to whom she should make a donation is played out through her engagement with another, does she or does she not look them in the eye. Silverman realizes that under her rationalizations is the fear of dissolution of her own body if she were also forced to live on the streets.

Silverman's arguments emphasizes the visual, in keeping with Freud's notion of the psyche as sign systems. Three further psychoanalytic concepts are introduced from the Seminars of Lacan to articulate how identification involves a theory of representation. They are, the *gaze*, the *screen* and the *look*. These are complex concepts, succinctly explained and referenced. The *screen* is the cultural filter which determines how we should appear to others; how the body should be healthy, whole, visibly gendered

FEMINIST REVIEW NO 62, SUMMER 1999

and exhibit the visual markers of sexual orientation, class, race, etc. The *gaze* belongs to those who see another through this screen. The *look* is the act of looking back at that other.

Silverman introduces her idea of the 'productive look', the conscious defiance of the screen. This act of looking back risks identifications with the non-ideal. This is the radical engagement with another which Silverman locates as necessary to the ethical imperative. The *screen* is not simply location of ideals, but also defines the abject, the body which is the wrong, size, shape, or colour. Silverman quotes Fanon who analyses how the screen may present the very opposite of an ideal. Of the gap between the proprioceptive ego and the body-ideals of the screen he wrote, 'It was no longer a question of being aware of my body in the third person but in a triple person' (Fanon, 1986[1952]: 112).

Where Lacan links the gaze to the camera, Silverman uses the camera as the primary trope for the *screen*. The films *Bildnis einer Trinkerin, Bilder der Welt und Inschrift des Krieges, Looking for Langston* and *Sans Soleil* make explicit the distinction between the *gaze* and the *look*. It is this tearing into a particular ideology which allows the viewer to recognize the productive *look* as the basis of political consciousness. Following Barthes, Silverman points out how the still photograph articulates the *gaze* through freezing the moment implying death as opposed to the more mobile acts of looking of the moving image. The *Untitled Film Stills* of Cindy Sherman demonstrate how the ideals inculcated by the *screen* are made visible through the framing, *mise-en-scène* and the disjunction between the position of the camera and the object of her look.

Kaja Silverman's text includes a far more sophisticated and broad-ranging analysis than I am able to convey here. What comes as a final surprise is the introduction of the British psychoanalyst D.W. Winnicott's concept of the 'good enough', an abridgment of his term the 'good enough mother'. Silverman uses this as a description of temperance, releasing us from unrealizable idealizing fantasy or fear bodily disintegration. Sherman then represents the 'good enough vamp' or 'good enough sophisticate'.

How then does this affect the ethical proposition? I admire any work which attempts to inspire a re-think of the politics of cinema and photography. The question remains open as to where we may then take our increased radical identifications, how are we to act without again acting *for* others? Silverman provides us with a 'good enough' plea for those involved in photography, film and video, 'to help us to see differently'.

Sharon Morris

Reference

Fanon, Frantz (1986[1952]) *Black Skin, White Masks*, London: Pluto Press.

FEMINIST REVIEW NO 62, SUMMER 1999, 0141-7789 PP. 142–152

1 Women and Revolution in South Yemen, **Molyneux**. Feminist Art Practice, **Davis & Goodal**. Equal Pay and Sex Discrimination, **Snell**. Female Sexuality in Fascist Ideology, **Macciocchi**. Charlotte Brontë's *Shirley*, **Taylor**. Christine Delphy, **Barrett & McIntosh**. OUT OF PRINT.

2 Summer Reading, **O'Rourke**. Disaggregation, **Campaign for Legal & Financial Independence** and **Rights of Women**. The Hayward Annual 1978, **Pollock**. Women and the Cuban Revolution, **Murray**. Matriarchy Study Group Papers, **Lee**. Nurseries in the Second World War, **Riley**.

3 English as a Second Language, **Naish**. Women as a Reserve Army of Labour, **Bruegel**. Chantal Akerman's films, **Martin**. Femininity in the 1950s, **Birmingham Feminist History Group**. On Patriarchy, **Beechey**. Board School Reading Books, **Davin**.

4 Protective Legislation, **Coyle**. Legislation in Israel, **Yuval-Davis**. On 'Beyond the Fragments', **Wilson**. Queen Elizabeth I, **Heisch**. Abortion Politics: **a dossier**. Materialist Feminism, **Delphy**.

5 Feminist Sexual Politics, **Campbell**. Iranian Women, **Tabari**. Women and Power, **Stacey & Price**. Women's Novels, **Coward**. Abortion, **Himmelweit**. Gender and Education, **Nava**. Sybilla Aleramo, **Caesar**. On 'Beyond the Fragments', **Margolis**.

6 'The Tidy House', **Steedman**. Writings on Housework, **Kaluzynska**. The Family Wage, **Land**. Sex and Skill, **Phillips & Taylor**. Fresh Horizons, **Lovell**. Cartoons, **Hay**.

7 Protective Legislation, **Humphries**. Feminists Must Face the Future, **Coultas**. Abortion in Italy, **Caldwell**. Women's Trade Union Conferences, **Breitenbach**. Women's Employment in the Third World, **Elson & Pearson**.

8 Socialist Societies Old and New, **Molyneux**. Feminism and the Italian Trade Unions, **Froggett & Torchi**. Feminist Approach to Housing in Britain, **Austerberry & Watson**. Psychoanalysis, **Wilson**. Women in the Soviet Union, **Buckley**. The Struggle within the Struggle, **Kimble**.

9 Position of Women in Family Law, **Brophy & Smart**. Slags or Drags, **Cowie & Lees**. The Ripper and Male Sexuality, **Hollway**. The Material of Male Power, **Cockburn**. Freud's *Dora*, **Moi**. Women in an Iranian Village, **Afshar**. New Office Technology and Women, **Morgall**.

10 Towards a Wages Strategy for Women, **Weir & McIntosh**. Irish Suffrage Movement, **Ward**. A Girls' Project and Some Responses to Lesbianism, **Nava**. The Case for Women's Studies, **Evans**. Equal Pay and Sex Discrimination, **Gregory**. Psychoanalysis and Personal Politics, **Sayers**.

11 Sexuality issue
Sexual Violence and Sexuality, **Coward**. Interview with Andrea Dworkin, **Wilson**. The Dyke, the Feminist and the Devil, **Clark**. Talking Sex, **English, Hollibaugh & Rubin**. Jealousy and Sexual Difference, **Moi**. Ideological Politics 1969–72, **O'Sullivan**. Womanslaughter in the Criminal Law, **Radford**. OUT OF PRINT.

12 ANC Women's Struggles, **Kimble & Unterhalter**. Women's Strike in Holland 1981, **de Bruijn & Henkes**. Politics of Feminist Research, **McRobbie**. Khomeini's Teachings on Women, **Afshar**. Women in the Labour Party 1906–1920, **Rowan**. Documents from the Indian Women's Movement, **Gothoskar & Patel**.

13 Feminist Perspectives on Sport, **Graydon**. Patriarchal Criticism and Henry James, **Kappeler**. The Barnard Conference on Sexuality, **Wilson**. Danger and Pleasure in Nineteenth Century Feminist Sexual Thought, **Gordon & Du Bois**. Anti-Porn: Soft Issue, Hard World, **Rich**. Feminist Identity and Poetic Tradition, **Montefiore**.

14 Femininity and its Discontents, **Rose**. Inside and Outside Marriage, **Gittins**. The Pro-family Left in the United States, **Epstein & Ellis**. Women's Language and Literature, **McKluskie**. The Inevitability of Theory, **Fildes**. The 150 Hours in Italy, **Caldwell**. Teaching Film, **Clayton**.

15 Women's Employment, **Beechey**. Women and Trade Unions, **Charles**. Lesbianism and Women's Studies, **Adamson**. Teaching Women's Studies at Secondary School, **Kirton**. Gender, Ethnic and Class Divisions, **Anthias & Yuval-Davis**. Women Studying or Studying Women, **Kelly & Pearson**. Girls, Jobs and Glamour, **Sherratt**. Contradictions in Teaching Women's Studies, **Phillips & Hurstfield**.

16 Romance Fiction, Female Sexuality and Class, **Light**. The White Brothel, **Kappeler**. Sadomasochism and Feminism, **France**. Trade Unions and Socialist Feminism, **Cockburn**. Women's Movement and the Labour Party, **Interview with Labour Party Feminists**. Feminism and 'The Family', **Caldwell**.

25 Difference: A Special Third World Women Issue, **Minh-ha**. Melanie Klein, Psychoanalysis and Feminism, **Sayers**. Rethinking Feminist Attitudes Towards Mothering, **Gieve**. EEOC v. Sears, Roebuck and Company: A Personal Account, **Kessler-Harris**. Poems, **Wood**. Academic Feminism and the Process of De-radicalization, **Currie & Kazi**. A Lover's Distance: A Photoessay, **Boffin**.

26 Resisting Amnesia: Feminism, Painting and Post-Modernism, **Lee**. The Concept of Difference, **Barrett**. The Weary Sons of Freud, **Clément**. Short Story, **Cole**. Taking the Lid Off: Socialist Feminism in Oxford, **Collette**. For and Against the European Left: Socialist Feminists Get Organized, **Benn**. Women and the State: A Conference of Feminist Activists, **Weir**.

27 **Women, feminism and the third term**
Women and Income Maintenance, **Lister**. Women in the Public Sector, **Phillips**. Can Feminism Survive a Third Term?, **Loach**. Sex in Schools, **Wolpe**. Carers and the Careless, **Doyal**. Interview with Diane Abbott, **Segal**. The Problem With No Name: Re-reading Friedan, **Bowlby**. Second Thoughts on the Second Wave, **Rosenfelt & Stacey**. Nazi Feminists?, **Gordon**.

28 **Family secrets: child sexual abuse**
Introduction to an Issue: Family Secrets as Public Drama, **McIntosh**. Challenging the Orthodoxy: Towards a Feminist Theory and Practice, **MacLeod & Saraga**. The Politics of Child Sexual Abuse: Notes from American History, **Gordon**. What's in a Name?: Defining Child Sexual Abuse, **Kelly**. A Case, **Anon**. Defending Innocence: Ideologies of Childhood, **Kitzinger**. Feminism and the Seductiveness of the 'Real Event', **Scott**. Cleveland and the Press: Outrage and Anxiety in the Reporting of Child Sexual Abuse, **Nava**. Child Sexual Abuse and the Law, **Woodcraft**. Poem, **Betcher**. Brixton Black Women's Centre: Organizing on Child Sexual Abuse, **Bogle**. Bridging the Gap: Glasgow Women's Support Project, **Bell & Macleod**. Claiming Our Status as Experts: Community Organizing, **Norwich Consultants on Sexual Violence**. Islington Social Services: Developing a Policy on Child Sexual Abuse, **Boushel & Noakes**. Developing a Feminist School Policy on Child Sexual Abuse, **O'Hara**. 'Putting Ideas into their Heads': Advising the Young, **Mills**. Child Sexual Abuse Crisis Lines: Advice for Our British Readers.

29 **Abortion: the international agenda**
Whatever Happened to 'A Woman's Right to Choose'?, **Berer**. More than 'A Woman's Right to Choose'?, **Himmelweit**. Abortion in the Republic of Ireland, **Barry**. Across the Water, **Irish Women's Abortion Support Group**. Spanish Women and the Alton Bill, **Spanish Women's Abortion Support Group**. The Politics of Abortion in Australia: Freedom, Church and State, **Coleman**. Abortion in Hungary, **Szalai**. Women and Population Control in China: Issues of Sexuality, Power and Control, **Hillier**. The Politics of Abortion in Nicaragua: Revolutionary Pragmatism – or Feminism in the Realm of Necessity?, **Molyneux**. Who Will Sing for Theresa?, **Bernstein**. She's Gotta Have It: The Representation of Black Female Sexuality on Film, **Simmonds**. Poems, **Gallagher**. Dyketactics for Difficult Times: A Review of the 'Homosexuality, Which Homosexuality?' Conference, **Franklin & Stacey**.

30 Capital, gender and skill

Women Homeworkers in Rural Spain, **Lever**. Fact and Fiction: George Egerton and Nellie Shaw, **Butler**. Feminist Political Organization in Iceland: Some Reflections on the Experience of Kwenna Frambothid, **Dominelli & Jonsdottir**. Under Western Eyes: Feminist Scholarship and Colonial Discourses, **Talpade Mohanty**. Bedroom Horror: The Fatal Attraction of *Intercourse*, **Merck**. AIDS: Lessons from the Gay Community, **Patton**. Poems, **Agbabi**.

31 The past before us: 20 years of feminism

Slow Change or No Change?: Feminism, Socialism and the Problem of Men, **Segal**. There's No Place Like Home: On the Place of Identity in Feminist Politics, **Adams**. New Alliances: Socialist-Feminism in the Eighties, **Harriss**. Other Kinds of Dreams, **Parmar**. Complexity, Activism, Optimism: Interview with **Angela Y. Davis**. To Be or Not To Be: The Dilemmas of Mothering, **Rowbotham**. Seizing Time and Making New: Feminist Criticism, Politics and Contemporary Feminist Fiction, **Lauret**. Lessons from the Women's Movement in Europe, **Haug**. Women in Management, **Coyle**. Sex in the Summer of '88, **Ardill & O'Sullivan**. Younger Women and Feminism, **Hobsbawm & Macpherson**. Older Women and Feminism, **Stacey; Curtis; Summerskill**.

32

'Those Who Die for Life Cannot Be Called Dead': Women and Human Rights Protest in Latin America, **Schirmer**. Violence Against Black Women: Gender, Race and State Responses, **Mama**. Sex and Race in the Labour Market, **Breugel**. The 'Dark Continent': Africa as Female Body in Haggard's Adventure Fiction, **Stott**. Gender, Class and the Welfare State: The Case of Income Security in Australia, **Shaver**. Ethnic Feminism: Beyond the Pseudo-Pluralists, **Gorelick**.

33

Restructuring the Woman Question: *Perestroika* and Prostitution, **Waters**. Contemporary Indian Feminism, **Kumar**. 'A Bit On the Side'?: Gender Struggles in South Africa, **Beall, Hassim and Todes**. 'Young Bess': Historical Novels and Growing Up, **Light**. Madeline Pelletier (1874–1939): The Politics of Sexual Oppression, **Mitchell**.

34 Perverse politics: lesbian issues

Pat Parker: A tribute, **Brimstone**. International Lesbianism: Letter from São Paulo, **Rodrigues**; Israel, **Pittsburgh**, Italy, **Fiocchetto**. The De-eroticization of Women's Liberation: Social Purity Movements and the Revolutionary Feminism of Sheila Jeffreys, **Hunt**. Talking About It: Homophobia in the Black Community, **Gomez & Smith**. Lesbianism and the Labour Party, **Tobin**. Skirting the Issue: Lesbian Fashion for the 1990s, **Blackman & Perry**. Butch/Femme Obsessions, **Ardill & O'Sullivan**. Archives: The Will to Remember, **Nestle**; International Archives, **Read**. Audre Lorde: Vignettes and Mental Conversations, **Lewis**. Lesbian Tradition, **Field**. Mapping: Lesbians, AIDS and Sexuality: An interview with Cindy Patton, **O'Sullivan**. Significant Others: Lesbians and Psychoanalytic Theory, **Hamer**. The Pleasure Threshold: Looking at Lesbian Pornography on Film, **Smyth**. Cartoon, **Charlesworth**. Voyages of the Valkyries: Recent Lesbian Pornographic Writing, **Dunn**.

35 Campaign Against Pornography, **Norden**. The Mothers' Manifesto and Disputes over 'Mutterlichkeit', **Chamberlayne**. Multiple Mediations: Feminist Scholarship in the Age of Multi-National Reception, **Mani**. Cagney and Lacey Revisited, **Alcock & Robson**. Cutting a Dash: The Dress of Radclyffe Hall and Una Troubridge, **Rolley**. Deviant Dress, **Wilson**. The House that Jill Built: Lesbian Feminist Organizing in Toronto, 1976–1980, **Ross**. Women in Professional Engineering: the Interaction of Gendered Structures and Values, **Carter & Kirkup**. Identity Politics and the Hierarchy of Oppression, **Briskin**. Poetry: **Bufkin, Zumwalt**.

36 'The Trouble Is It's Ahistorical': The Problem of the Unconscious in Modern Feminist Theory, **Minsky**. Feminism and Pornography, **Ellis, O'Dair Tallmer**. Who Watches the Watchwomen? Feminists Against Censorship, **Rodgerson & Semple**. Pornography and Violence: What the 'Experts' Really Say, **Segal**. The Woman In My Life: Photography of Women, **Nava**. Splintered Sisterhood: Antiracism in a Young Women's Project, **Connolly**. Woman, Native, Other, **Parmar** interviews **Trinh T. Minh-ha**. Out But Not Down: Lesbians' Experience of Housing, **Edgerton**. Poems: **Evans Davies, Toth, Weinbaum**. Oxford Twenty Years On: Where Are We Now?, **Gamman & O'Neill**. The Embodiment of Ugliness and the Logic of Love: The Danish Redstockings Movement, **Walter**.

37 Theme issue: Women, religion and dissent
Black Women, Sexism and Racism: Black or Antiracist Feminism?, **Tang Nain**. Nursing Histories: Reviving Life in Abandoned Selves, **McMahon**. The Quest for National Identity: Women, Islam and the State in Bangladesh, **Kabeer**. Born Again Moon: Fundamentalism in Christianity and the Feminist Spirituality Movement, **McCrickard**. Washing our Linen: One Year of Women Against Fundamentalism, **Connolly**. Siddiqui on *Letter to Christendom*, **Bard** on *Generations of Memories*, **Patel** on *Women Living Under Muslim Laws Dossiers 1–6*, Poem, **Kay**. More Cagney and Lacey, **Gamman**.

38 The Modernist Style of Susan Sontag, **McRobbie**. Tantalizing Glimpses of Stolen Glances: Lesbians Take Photographs, **Fraser and Boffin**. Reflections on the Women's Movement in Trinidad, **Mohammed**. Fashion, Representation and Femininity, **Evans & Thornton**. The European Women's Lobby, **Hoskyns**. Hendessi on *Law of Desire: Temporary Marriage in Iran*, **Kaveney** on *Mercy*.

39 Shifting territories: feminism & Europe
Between Hope and Helplessness: Women in the GDR, **Dölling**. Where Have All the Women Gone? Women and the Women's Movement in East Central Europe, **Einhorn**. The End of Socialism in Europe – A New Challenge For Socialist Feminism? **Haug**. The Second 'No': Women in Hungary, **Kiss**. The Citizenship Debate: Women, the State and Ethnic Processes, **Yuval-Davis**. Fortress Europe and Migrant Women, **Morokvasíc**. Racial Equality and 1992, **Dummett**. Questioning *Perestroika*: A Socialist Feminist Interrogation, **Pearson**. Postmodernism and its Discontents, **Soper**. Feminists and Socialism: After the Cold War, **Kaldor**. Socialism Out of the Common Pots, **Mitter**. 1989 and All That, **Campbell**. In Listening

Mode, **Cockburn. Women in Action: Country by Country:** The Soviet Union; Yugoslavia; Czechoslavakia; Hungary; Poland. **Reports:** International Gay and Lesbian Association: Black Women and Europe 1992.

40 Fleurs du Mal or Second-Hand Roses?: Nathalie Barney, Romaine Brooks, and the 'Originality of the Avant-Garde', **Elliott & Wallace.** Poem, **Tyler-Bennett.** Feminism and Motherhood: An American 'Reading' **Snitow.** Qualitative Research, Appropriation of the 'Other' and Empowerment, **Opie.** Disabled Women and the Feminist Agenda, **Begum.** Postcard From the Edge: Thoughts on the 'Feminist Theory: An International Debate' Conference at Glasgow University, July 1991, **Radstone.** Review Essay, **Munt.**

41 Editorial. The Selling of HRT: Playing on the Fear Factor, **Worcester & Whatley.** The Cancer Drawings of Catherine Arthur, **Sebastyen.** Ten years of Women's Health 1982–92, **James.** AIDS Activism: Women and AIDS activism in Victoria, Australia, **Mitchell.** A Woman's Subject, **Friedli.** HIV and the Invisibility of Women: Is there a Need to Redefine AIDS?, **Scharf & Toole.** Lesbians Evolving Health Care: Cancer and AIDS, **Winnow.** Now is the Time for Feminist Criticism: A Review of *Asinimali!*, **Steinberg.** Ibu or the Beast?: Gender Interests in Two Indonesian Women's Organizations, **Wieringa.** Reports on Motherlands: Symposium on African, Carribean and Asian Women's Writing, **Smart.** The European Forum of Socialist Feminists, **Bruegel.** Review Essay, **Gamman.**

42 Feminist fictions
Editorial. Angela Carter's *The Bloody Chamber* and the Decolonization of Feminine Sexuality, **Makinen.** Feminist Writing: Working with Women's Experience, **Haug.** Three Aspects of Sex in Marge Piercy's *Fly Away Home*, **Hauser.** Are They Reading Us? Feminist Teenage Fiction, **Bard.** Sexuality in Lesbian Romance Fiction, **Hermes.** A Psychoanalytic Account for Lesbianism, **Castendyk.** Mary Wollstonecraft and the Problematic of Slavery, **Ferguson.** Reviews.

43 Issues for feminism
Family, Motherhood and Zulu Nationalism: The Politics of the Inkatha Women's Brigade, **Hassim.** Postcolonial Feminism and the Veil: Thinking the Difference, **Abu Odeh.** Feminism, the Menopause and Hormone Replacement Therapy, **Lewis.** Feminism and Disability, **Morris.** 'What is Pornography?': An Analysis of the Policy Statement of the Campaign Against Pornography and Censorship, **Smith.** Reviews.

44 Nationalisms and national identities
Women, Nationalism and Islam in Contemporary Political Discourse in Iran, **Yeganeh.** Feminism, Citizenship and National Identity, **Curthoys.** Remapping and Renaming: New Cartographies of Identity, Gender and Landscape in Ireland, **Nash.** Rap Poem: Easter 1991, **Medbh.** Family Feuds: Gender, Nationalism and the Family, **McClintock.** Women as Activists; Women as Symbols: A Study of the Indian Nationalist Movement, **Thapar.** Gender, Nationalisms and National Identities: Bellagio Symposium Report, **Hall.** Culture or Citizenship? Notes from the Gender and Colonialism Conference, Galway, Ireland, May 1992, **Connolly.** Reviews.

FEMINIST REVIEW NO 62, SUMMER 1999

61 Snakes and Ladders: Reviewing Feminisms at Century's End

Editorial Snakes and Ladders: Reviewing Feminisms at Century's End, **Catherine Hall, Sue O'Sullivan, Ann Phoenix, Merl Storr, Lyn Thomas, Annie Whitehead**. The Scent of Memory: Strangers, Our Own and Others **Avtar Brah**. Writing from Experience: The Place of the Personal in French Feminist Writing, **Lyn Thomas and Emma Webb**. Fragments around Philippe V., **Annie Ernaux**. 'Gone are the Days': Bisexual Perspectives on Lesbian/Feminist Literary Theory, **Anne Kaloski Naylor**. Feminist Recoveries in *My Father's House*, **Christine Clegg**. Sexual Abuse and Troubled Feminism: A Reply to Camille Guy, **Chris Atmore**. What a Difference a Decade Makes: *Coming to Power* and *The Second Coming*, **Sue O'Sullivan**. *No Title*, 1992 **Nicky West**. An Interview with Nicky West on *No Title*, **Lyn Thomas**. Women's Studies: Between a Rock and a Hard Place or Just Another Cell in the Beehive, **Helen Crowley**. Reviews

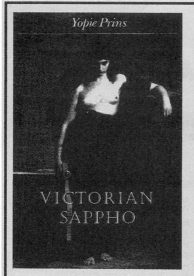

Feminist Review is published three times a year. It is edited by a Collective which is supported by a group of Corresponding Editors.

The Collective: Amal Treacher, Avtar Brah, Annie E. Coombes, Dot Griffiths, Helen Crowley, Lucy Bland, Lyn Thomas, Merl Storr, Pam Alldred, Rita Rupal, Sharon Morris, Vicki Bertram.

This Issue was edited by: Vicki Bertram.

Corresponding Editors: Ailbhe Smyth, Ann Curthoys, Hala Shukrallah, Kum-Kum Bhavnani, Jacqui Alexander, Lidia Curti, Meera Kosambi, Patricia Mohammed, Zarina Maharaj.

Correspondence and advertising

Contributions, books for review and editorial correspondence should be sent to: *Feminist Review*, c/o Women's Studies, University of North London, 166–220 Holloway Road, London N7 8DB.

For a complete and up-to-date guide to Taylor & Francis Group's journals and books publishing programmes, and details on advertising in our journals, write to: New Fetter Lane, London EC4P 4EE or visit our website: http:/www.tandf.co.uk

Notes for Contributors

Authors should submit four copies of their work to: *Feminist Review*, c/o Women's Studies, University of North London, 166–220 Holloway Road, London N7 8DB.

We assume that you will keep a copy of your work. Submission of work to *Feminist Review* will be taken to imply that it is original, unpublished work, which is not under consideration for publication elsewhere. All work is subject to a system of anonymous peer review. All work is refereed by at least two external (non-Collective) referees.

Please note that we cannot accept unsolicited book reviews.

Typeset by Type Study, Scarborough
Printed in Great Britain by Bell & Bain Ltd, Glasgow

ISSN 0141-7789

Please send all correspondence to:
Feminist Review
c/o Women's Studies
University of North London
166–220 Holloway Road
London N7 8DB